MY GREAT, GREAT, GRANDFATHER'S JOURNEY
TO
AN ISLAND OF FREEDOM IN THE MIDDLE OF SLAVERY

Col Lafayette Jones, Jr.

JENLAF Publishing
102 Flintlock Road
Williamsburg, Virginia 23185
PH: 757-565-2724

Copyright © June 2007 by Col Lafayette Jones, Jr.
Reprint April 2012

All rights reserved including the right to reproduce or be stored in a retrieval system manually, electronically, mechanically, photocopied or transmitted by any form or means. International copyright is applied. The use of this book or any portion thereof, in any form or by any means without the expressed written permission of JENLAF Publishing is prohibited. Comments used in Oral Histories are individualized and copyrighted.

Library of Congress   2008932645
Cataloging in Publication Data

Col Lafayette Jones, Jr. 2007
    My Great, Great, Grandfather's Journey
To An Island of Freedom In The Middle of Slavery

ISBN 978-0-615-22337

Book Design and Cover   Col Lafayette Jones, Jr.
Production Coordinator
Cover Illustration

TABLE OF CONTENTS

FOREWORD v
DEDICATION ix
ACKNOWLEDGEMENT xi
INTRODUCTION xiii

I. The Arrival 1

II. The Enslaved and the Freedmen 11

III. Education and Religion 27

IV. Hot Water 35

V. The Jones Family and Oral Histories 47

Conclusion 111

Time will tell
   - Anonymous

FOREWORD

Only once in a great while does a book appear as a historical work characterized by fresh insight, vibrant writing, and original historical knowledge. *My Great, Great Grandfather's Journey* is a book that permeates with all of these features and more. In this book Col Lafayette Jones, Jr., sketches the beginning of slavery in America and eases into a historical revelation of his family's life as free blacks during the period preceding the civil war. He also provides a revealing insight into the development of the Hotwater Tract, known today as Freedom Park, one of the first organized free black communities in America. With great subtlety, he introduces fresh information by the use of oral histories and first hand historical fact about the residents of this free black community that originated in 1803.

I first met Col Jones in January 2000 when he addressed the Board of Supervisors James City County, Virginia, during an open meeting session. Col Jones addressed the commission and gave a heart rendering speech about the new district park that was under consideration for James City County. During his speech, he stated that the land where the park was proposed was the site of one of the oldest free black settlements in the nation, that the story of this free black community was untold, and that the park should emphasize the role that the community played in developing the culture in this area. He asked the board of supervisors to consider the importance of the area to the local black populace who were descendents of these early African Americans, and that action to preserve it as a monument to these early Americans be taken.

When the Division of Parks and Recreation made a public announcement in 2003 that they were seeking a name for the new district park, Col Jones again appeared before the Board of Supervisors and asked that they consider the name "Freedom Park." Through his efforts, he was able to present signed petitions by the local residents and church congregations supporting his recommendation. After consideration of 26 different names submitted to the Board of Supervisors, the name selected was "Freedom Park". Ned Cheely, Director of Parks and Recreation, said, "After careful consideration of all names submitted "Freedom Park" really stands out above the rest. The name resounds with the history of that land and demonstrates the quest for liberty and freedom".

Freedom Park sits on land that is rich with history and has played a significant part in the shaping our country. Not only is it the site of this free black settlement, it also is the site of the June 26, 1781, Revolutionary War Battle of Spencer's Ordinary, and the site of a homestead dating back to 1680-1730.

In 2003, Col Jones received a James City County Historical Preservation Award. Only persons who have made a significant contribution to the county's history receive this award. Since then, he has been instrumental in the planning and development of Freedom Park. Col Jones is Chairman of the James City County Historical

Commission and has been a member since 2003. Recently, he has worked as a consultant with the Department of Parks and Recreation, the Jamestown Foundation, and several other historical foundations in the area. - **Reverend Jay T. Harrison, Sr.**
Former President, Board of Supervisors James City County, Virginia

DEDICATION

This book, dedicated to the memory of my Grandfather, Mr. George A. Jones, and the brave free African-Americans and former slaves who resided in the Hot Water Tract, tells the story about a Free Black Settlement established in 1803, near Williamsburg, Virginia. These free black men and women lived in a self-sustaining black community of tradesmen and farmers that coexisted alongside slavery for more than 60 years.

George A. Jones 1870-1973
Courtesy - L. Jones

x

ACKNOWLEDGEMENT

The inspiration and support that I have received in the writing of this book has been phenomenal! Many of the people contacted as sources for information became excited about having an opportunity to share their knowledge with me. Their excitement served as motivation for me to pursue the writing of this book and reinforced my belief in the value of recorded African-American history. One of the most important facts relating to that history was that not all blacks had been slaves from birth to death.

Acknowledgement is given to the James City County Board of Commissioners, James City County Historical Commission, and members of the County Parks and Recreation Division who provided resources for the compilation of historical and archaeological services relating to the Hot Water Tract (Freedom Park). Also acknowledged is Martha McCartney, local historian and author, who researched the history of some of the slaves freed by William Ludwell-Lee, owner of the Green Springs Plantation. William Ludwell-Lee was the person responsible for the establishment of this early free black settlement on a portion of his property.

My major thanks are afforded my grandfather and other relatives who helped in the development of oral histories relating to the Hot Water Tract. Additionally, a special acknowledgement is given to the hard working African-Americans that wisely used their humble beginnings to develop their free community and instill in their offspring certain values demonstrated by many of their descendents.

INTRODUCTION

The story of my great, great grandfather's journey will enable me to help correct, as near as possible, some of the misconceptions about African American history in the area where my family lived in the state of Virginia as freemen during eighteenth century America. The history of Hot Water lies buried below the ground or in the limited writings and oral traditions of peoples who passed through this site. To gain more accurate information relative to Hot Water, archaeologists and other scholars have relied on limited resources such as documents, images, and artifacts created by people who lived and worked there.

If I could turn back the clock to the days when my great, great grandfather was a little boy, we could learn a lot more about Hot Water and its surrounding areas such as James City County, Virginia, Green Springs Plantation and Williamsburg. Much of the story about Hot Water evolves around these areas. Hot Water is located in the suburbs of Williamsburg, Virginia, at the intersection of Longhill and Centerville Roads. Today its name is Freedom Park.

The purpose of this book is to provide new information on a great "story" related to my family and the free black settlement at Hot Water. Most of the information is based on local and state records, interviews, and articles written by renowned historians.

Many historians/researchers agree that two of the difficulties in assessing historical roles of African Americans during the period of slavery in America occur because their real contributions are negatively portrayed or neglected completely.

L. Douglas Wilder, Chairman, Board of Directors of the United States National Slave Museum, and former Governor of Virginia, confirmed this when he recently stated,

"By telling their stories (former slaves) we offer hope for equality, tolerance and solutions to the pressing slavery-rooted issues of our society today."

The assumption that the original Jamestown colonists had never seen blacks is obviously untrue. Africans and their descendants have shared a documented history in the development of Europe since medieval times and in the America's dating back to the late 1400's. They performed such duties as interpreters, soldiers, sailors, navigators, scouts, and ship's captain. Prominent historians have reported that when Christopher Columbus discovered the Americas his navigator was of African descent and men of African descent commanded two of his three ships. Black Africans were among the first to encounter Native Americans when the Spanish conquistadors arrived in the new world.

Reportedly, the arrival of approximately 20 Africans at Jamestown, Virginia, in August 1619 marks the beginning of Slavery in America. This too is erroneous because Slavery did not exist under English law at that time, but indentured servitude did. Most indentured servants had a contract for a specified number of years, but if there was no contract, the law did not set a limit on the length of servitude. According to the law at that time, most of those early African-Americans at Jamestown became free men after their term of servitude.

According to Paul Heinegg, a highly regarded genealogist,
"There is a record of at least one of them taking up some land and paying the passage of some white servants from England, thus acquiring indentured servants of his own".[1]

Not too many Americans realize that there was once a time when blacks had white indentured servants. There are descendents of these early African-Americans, whose ancestors (in that line, at least) were never slaves, still living in the Williamsburg area.

It took years for American law to create our "peculiar institution" of slavery. When a person said he owned "slaves", in the early 1600s, he was referring to his indentured servants, and they could be European, African, or Native American.[2] Laws gradually extended the term of servitude for blacks and shortened it for whites. Eventually servitude became a lifetime obligation for blacks. Other laws forbade black-white and slave-free marriages, and required that the children of slaves also be the property of the master, making American slavery unlike slavery in ancient Rome or in Africa, where this was not the case.[3]

As noted by Noble H. Pace in his article, <u>One of America's Oldest Immigrant Families</u>:

"American children are all taught the story of the Pilgrims and how their ship, the Mayflower, landed at Plymouth Rock during the summer of 1620. They also are taught that one year later the Governor of the Plymouth Colony proclaimed a day of "thanksgiving" to celebrate the Pilgrim's first harvest in America. American children also are taught that the Jamestown residents were startled when they saw the first black slaves at Jamestown."[4]

Yet, the arrival of African Americans at Jamestown, more than a year before the Mayflower arrived at Plymouth Rock is rarely documented or taught. Jamestown, established in 1607, was the first permanent English Settlement in North America.

CHAPTER I

THE ARRIVAL

The following is the story of the first slave ship coming to Jamestown, Virginia, and the subsequent result of its arrival. Many historians have presented similar evidence of the first arrival, however, it is important here to briefly consider some of the agreed upon background that led to the entry of Africans at Jamestown and the resulting institution of slavery in America.

Writing in "The Shaping of Black America" Lerone Bennett, Jr., states,

"This drama which is known as the African Slave Trade had been going on for more than 100 years when the Virginia colony was founded in 1607. By that time, European slave traders had transported tens of thousands of Blacks to the New World to work in the Spanish West Indies, Brazil, Cuba and other colonies... In the years immediately preceding the Jamestown Landing, the slave trade and colonization movement were dominated by the Spanish, Portuguese and Dutch."[5]

The slave trade developed into a very large business in the 17th and 18th centuries and primarily Dutch, French and English companies controlled it. The Dutch West Indies Company, organized in 1621, immediately did everything possible to control the slave market.[6] Many of its attempts at cornering the market failed. Thus, by the end of the 17th century its position had declined considerably. Despite its loss of control caused by bitter wars with the British, the Dutch influence continued over much of West Africa and many Dutch traders made fortunes in the slave trade. England did not become a major slave trading power until around 1672 when it formed the Royal African Company. The king of England was a charter member.

Prior to that time, the English colonies relied upon privateers or "freebooters" to obtain its illegal work force from Africa. Opportunists such as Captain Daniel Elfrith, of the Man-of-war "Treasurer", Captain Arthur Guy, of the ship "Fortune", Captain John Powell, of the ship "Hopewell", and Captain John Colyn Jope, who commanded the "Lion" a Dutch Privateer, conducted raids against the Spanish and Portuguese slave ships. Some of the Dutch privateers shipped Africans to New York where they were purchased and resold to the southern-most English colonies. The raids by the "freebooters" were restricted primarily to Spanish and Portuguese slave ships.

In April of 1619, the Governor of the Jamestown Colony, Sir George Yeardley, sent two ships, the Treasurer and the Lion, on a supposed "routine trading voyage". In fact, the true purpose of these ships was to act as privateers or pirate ships to conduct raids against Spanish and Portuguese shipping in the West Indies. The two heavily armed vessels captured a Portuguese merchant-slave ship named the "San Juan Bautista" and confiscated the ship's cargo. Part of the cargo was approximately 100 Africans enroute to the Caribbean as slaves.[7] The Dutch Warship returned to Old Point Comfort in August 1619 with its load of captured goods and the Africans. Shortly after the return of the Dutch ship to America, the Treasurer also returned to America.[8] Soon thereafter, the Treasurer set sail for Bermuda with twenty-nine of the original 100 Africans stolen from the Portuguese. Later Jamestown became the official port of entry for new slaves.

Governor Sir George Yeardley and the colony's wealthiest resident, a merchant named Abraham Peirsey traded for most of the Africans. Following the trade, smaller vessels smuggled approximately 20 of the stolen Africans from Old Point Comfort to Jamestown.[9] Because slavery in the North American colonies was illegal, they were relocated to the Wyandotte Indian Camp in Charles Cittie (today's Charles City County) where they were held until their status as indentured servants could be established.

The Portuguese had considered the Africans to be slaves. However, because slavery had been eliminated as a classification in English law, the Africans had to be classified legally as indentured servants. Based on a Virginia Census taken in March of 1619, which may not be entirely reliable, there were already 32 blacks (15 men and 17 women) in the service of Jamestown planters.[10] This was prior to the August arrival of the Dutch ship. If the March census is accurate, it is possible that these earlier blacks migrated as free people from England or the Caribbean.

4

There are indications that, after several years of servitude, some of the Africans brought to Jamestown as indentured servants eventually obtained their freedom after seven or ten years of servitude. Some even considered themselves yeomen. However, unlike most white indentured servants who voluntarily contracted their services for a specified period, some of these Africans may not have been given this option. It is possible that some of them remained in servitude for the rest of their lives. Indeed, by 1625, the Jamestown census listed ten slaves.

According to noted historians, the number of African slaves in the colonies would increase by the thousands over the next few decades. There were circumstances during the 17th century that caused most of the first Africans arriving in the Americas to come from Angola, Africa.

The Africans brought a wide variety of skills and occupations to the colonies such as household workers, sailors, accountants, medical assistants, ironworkers, carpenters, pottery makers and bricklayers. Many of them were specialized in architectural design, agriculture, decorative arts, musical forms and music. Their work, which still marks the landscape today, helped shape American cultural styles.

Despite reports by some early historians that the blacks brought to America were a savage and godless people, history has shown that the Africans brought to this country had a deep sense of family and communal responsibility. They brought with them African languages, religious beliefs, styles of worship and, above all, their culture.

5

Typical Virginia Cotton Field– Pre-1865
Underwood & Underwood
Library of Congress P & P Division

However, it is interesting to note that a vast number of the Black Africans brought to this country worked primarily as agricultural laborers. This was because they already possessed extensive knowledge and experience in cultivating crops grown in North and West Africa such as rice, cotton and sugar. Their skills became the basis for the economic development of the southern states. The descendents of these first African Americans have made significant contributions to the growth of this country in all areas of knowledge.

"It is estimated that by 1750 more than 40 percent of Virginia's population was African American. However, the largest concentration of blacks was in South Carolina where it was estimated that at least 60 percent of its population was African American."[11]

Their experience in cattle herding, rice growing, water navigation and forestation was the best. Their skills in these areas were well known by the Europeans. For example, in South Carolina and Georgia, where the most profitable crop was rice, the white planters utilized the rice growing skills of the slaves from Senegambia, an area located in West Africa. Their cultivation of rice made it a major crop for exportation to Europe. The same held true for the growing of tobacco in Maryland, Virginia, the Carolinas and Georgia.

When one takes a general look at the enslaved community that surrounded "free areas" similar to where my great, great, grandfather grew up in the late nineteenth century, a vision of cruel, harsh reality comes into view. In reality, it was a community based on both African and European patterns and culture. European activities were incorporated into the plantation system of control and Africans were conditioned to adapt for survival. As stated by Lerone Bennett, Jr., The Shaping of Black America:

"Although a number of white authorities question the existence of an African-influenced slave community, the authority of evidence is more imposing. The evidence comes from three sources: the testimony of slaves, the testimony of slave owners, and the testimony of slave behavior as objectified in events, folklore, and art. Most of the evidence, even the evidence of hostile witnesses, enables us to see that the slaves had a community of feeling, recognition of special obligations, and an "us" perspective."[12]

Commenting further on the psychological impact of the American Slave system, Lerone Bennett, quoting Alexis Tocqueville's "Study of America" said,

"The only means by which the ancients maintained slavery were fetters and death: the Americans of the South of the Union have discovered more intellectual insecurities for the duration of their power. They have employed their despotism and their violence against the human mind."[13]

Many efforts to devoid the slaves of their original culture, including language and religion were attempted. The main purpose of their existence was one of production that aided in the economic growth of the plantation. Whereas a slave's day began at sunrise and usually ended at sunset, living and working conditions were extremely regimented. Men, women, old and young worked the same schedule. Many fall harvests involved work during the night hours. As slaves struggled to survive in inferior living conditions or slave quarters, they tried to maintain some type of family unit. They also practiced and preserved many aspects of their native culture such as the preparation of food and the cultivation of food for their consumption.

More specifically, despite the difficulty of slave labor, there were some advantages to working on the plantation compared to working in the city or urban area. However, the disadvantages far out weighed the advantages. The plantation slave was more likely to be sold or transferred to another location than slaves in an urban environment. They also were more likely to incur brutal, repressive and sometimes sadistic punishments because they were not as highly valued as the urban or household slave.

Urban slaves generally were unable to form close family units because they normally were hired-out or had jobs where they worked independently of other slaves and people of a different gender. Most domestic jobs employed females that were required to live in lofts or rooms in the owner's house where they had little or no privacy. Most of the male slaves worked as coachmen, waiters, butlers, gardeners and tradesmen. They often lived in the barn or other area unique to their work place. Work conditions for plantation slaves were dictated by the season or harvest time, but the urban slave's work was dictated by the task and could be required at any time.

Although the jobs of urban slaves were quite tedious, they ate better food, had a greater opportunity to travel and move about the city or urban area, dressed better, and had better living conditions. They often served as messengers and go-betweens for the master and the field hands. Sometimes they were hired out to the plantation owners to oversee the plantation slaves. Because of their freedom to randomly move about they were more likely to hear information discussed by the master and his associates. As such, the urban and city slaves were able to develop an innate ability to anticipate the master's reaction and probable course of action to the latest news and political situations. Sometimes the city slaves were in a better position to improve their condition, but they still had considerable fear of the master's ability to cause them anguish and subject them to severe punishments for the slightest reason, thus their environment was one of uncertainty. In many cases, the house servants were born and bred in the family that owned them. Even when this was not the case, the constant association of the slaves and their master's family naturally led to an attachment that insured good treatment.

The position of the field hand was very different. There were no humanizing influences for those who labored on large plantations; nor did public opinion control abuse. The field hands were left to the whims of the "white overseer and the Negro-driver."

10

CHAPTER II

The Enslaved and the Freedmen

During the time in which my great, great, grandfather lived, some of the slaves lived and acted as free persons of color and acquired real estate and other property. Little has been documented about these "virtually free slaves."[14] However, this is not surprising since words revealing the existence of a free black populace in the midst of a slave society would have caused widespread slave revolts throughout the nation.

Since the livelihoods of these "virtually free slaves" depended upon secrecy or deception, there had to be a tacit illegal agreement with a prominent white slaveholder and free Blacks in order for them to survive in a slave society. Therefore, it is extremely difficult even to identify, much less uncover information about such slaves, unless it is obtained from oral history. Owners were reluctant to acknowledge that bondsmen in their charge roamed about unsupervised, undermining the controls so necessary for the slave system to function properly.[15]

The unsuspecting foreign traveler, or northern visitor, or southern defender of slavery, believed these blacks to be free Negroes; and these virtually free slaves refused to admit, much less advertise, their situation.[16] Consequently, the journals of the slaveholding class, descriptions by outside visitors, writings of white southerners, and to a large extent even the narratives, recollections, and autobiographical reminiscences of blacks themselves, contain only fleeting references to slaves who exercised many of the privileges of free men and women.[17]

In Williamsburg, many of the slaves and legally free blacks found employment as farmers, masons, barbers, confectioners, laborers hostlers, carpenters, carriage men, wagon drivers, builders, Longshoremen, Fishermen and blacksmiths.[18] After the Revolutionary War in 1776 and the emancipation of slaves from Green Springs Plantation, in 1803, the number of nominal slaves and legally free blacks grew steadily in Williamsburg and other nearby cities.

Many of these free blacks, including members of my family, transported goods such as tobacco, animal hides, sugar, brandy, rum, pottery, nails, glass, cookware, tea, coffee, molasses, raisins, wines, logwood, tin, and other commodities along the James River from Richmond to Cape Henry.[19] The hiring out of free blacks and trusted slaves following the American Revolution became quite prevalent in the Upper South.[20]

As ports and shipping points along the Virginia coast and the inland waterways began to grow, a demand for commercial items such as meat, dairy products, vegetables, fruit, and most of all, skilled Craftsmen increased. As a result, many of these businesses began to hire free blacks and trusted slaves who were "hired-out" by their owners. They were hired as cooks, domestics, and freight handlers. White

Businessmen then subleased them to other businesses for a profit. For example, one young entrepreneur named Cook, hired William Richeson, a slave, from his mistress and then hired him out in Memphis, Tennessee, to work on a boat."[21]

Bringing in the Tobacco Crop
Yorktown Foundation

Many whites considered the practice of slave hires as being dangerous to social stability and a threat to the concept of slavery. Worse still, some slave owners found it convenient to allow their bondspersons to hire-out themselves, negotiate their own wages, and to come and go as they pleased; as long as they paid the master his share of their wages. These slaves then became virtually free.[22] Whatever a skilled Craftsman could make beyond the sum he owed his master was his to keep. Although self-hire became common around the Chesapeake in the years after the American Revolution, virtually free blacks were in most large southern towns and cities. However, the demands of an expanding cotton and tobacco economy kept the practice from developing in the interior of the Lower South. In the countryside, slaves remained subjected to the restrictions and horrible conditions that existed at their masters' isolated farms and plantations.[23]

Whether they hired themselves out or leased by their masters, the law required slaves in every southern state to return to their masters' homes at the end of each working day, but many did not, and some simply could not. Cities like Norfolk, Richmond, Yorktown, and Williamsburg were compact enough that hired bondmen could usually return to their owners' houses each night. Slaves who hired their time by the week or month sometimes found it necessary to find a room near their place of temporary employment.[24]

Some early historians have concluded that this practice of hiring out slaves led to the slave resistance displayed in some of the larger southern cities. Others have noted that selling one's wares at a Sunday market increased the psychological distance between master and slave. The ability of large numbers of urbanized African Americans to operate in nearly independent back alley communities with other black Craftsmen challenged slavery by creating a sense of collective self-sufficiency. One urban bondman,

John Williams, complained that his "rights were violated" when his legal owner, Joseph Winston, continued to assign him tasks despite the fact that he had been hired to John Enders for the year. "Another visitor to the South commented on a slave who had so little contact with his master that he saw him only at Christmas, when he paid his share of hiring money, gave an account of his travels and successes, said how well he was, and how well he was doing."[25]

" In one curious case along Virginia's James River, hired slaves who worked at the Buffalo Forge iron works were not only paid a cash wage, some of them opened savings accounts in their own names."[26] Virginia bankers clearly felt uncomfortable about paying interest on money belonging to slaves but, if local authorities paid little attention, they typically allowed business to override racial feelings.[27]

By the late 1850's, some slaves, such as the industrious Sam Williams, were earning overtime of more than $100 annually[28]. Sam and his wife Nancy may have been saving in hopes of purchasing their freedom or that of their children, but the fact remains that they reportedly had disposable income in their savings account. This may suggest that they were able financially to meet their material needs and did not need to exhaust their finances to purchase food and clothing.

Paul Heinegg, in his book: <u>Free African Americans in North Carolina, Virginia and South Carolina</u>, Publisher: Clearfield Company, 2001, wrote:

> "Most of the Free African-American Families of Virginia and North Carolina who originated in Virginia really became free in the 17th - 18th-century, long before chattel slavery and racism fully developed in

the United States. When the first Africans arrived in Virginia, they joined a society that was divided between a master and white servant. They joined the same households with white servants, working, eating, sleeping, getting drunk, and running away together."[29]

Most of the free black families were the descendants of white women who had children by black men. According to some noted historians, the number of Free African American families who descended from white male slave owners was less than one percent of the total free black population prior to 1680.[30] Some of their descendants formed the tri-racial groups and communities of Virginia, North Carolina, Tennessee, Kentucky, Ohio, Louisiana and South Carolina.[31]

By 1670, free blacks had moved to most of the areas along the coast of Virginia and North Carolina. Free blacks also moved to the western parts of Virginia and North Carolina where they established sizable homesteads adjacent to the white settlers. The white settlers had no difficulty in accepting these new arrivals because they provided an additional source of security for the western frontier. As time moved on, free blacks began to develop their own settlements in some areas. However, as the percentage of freed African-Americans increased, so did tension between African-Americans and slaveholders.

As more and more Africans gained their freedom and began pursuing legal courses of action to guarantee their rights, an imbalance started to appear between the percentage of black indentured servants and white indentured servants. In order to reverse this trend, the legislature began passing a series of laws to diminish the rights of free blacks and eventually designated slavery as the appropriate condition for most African-Americans.[32]

New Towne in the 1660s. By Keith Rocco
NPS COLORADO

These laws were enacted out of fear. Many of the white settlers felt intimidated and threatened by the new order of free African Americans and their accomplishments, especially the wealthy landowners, Businessmen and clergy. In many instances, this legislation led to the murder, kidnapping and selling of free African-Americans into slavery.[33] This was true especially after the enactment of the Fugitive Slave Law that required all states to return runaway slaves to their owners.

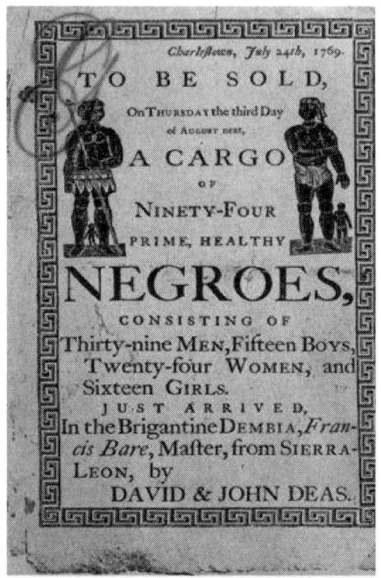

Slave Sale Notice
Granger Collection, NY

Enactment and Codification of the Slave Laws

To understand fully the ordeals faced by African Americans, both free and slave, knowledge of the laws that created this violation of basic freedoms is important. Beginning in 1660, a concerted effort was made by the Virginia General Assembly to replace white servants with African slaves. The replacement of white servants continued for more than a century and did not reach its completion until the late 1700s.

In 1670, the Virginia Assembly started making new laws to disenfranchise and stop the recognition of achievements made by free African-Americans.[34] The new laws also prohibited Free African Americans and Indians from owning white servants.

In 1691, the Virginia assembly prohibited the freeing of slaves unless they were transported out of the colony. These laws also prohibited interracial marriage and ordered that all illegitimate, mixed-race children of white women be bound out as indentured servants for a period of 30 years.

In 1705, the assembly passed a law that all but eliminated the ability of slaves to earn their freedom by ordering that all farm stock of slaves be seized and sold by the church Wardens of the parish where animals such as horses, cattle, or hogs would be sold.[35] After the approval of this law, many additional laws were written to eliminate all rights of African American Slaves while significantly suppressing the rights of Free African-Americans. The laws became so restrictive that it reduced the rights of Free Blacks to little more than those of the slave.[36]

The first documented "20 and odd" Blacks that arrived in Jamestown, Virginia, in August of 1619, were not known to have been enslaved immediately (sic).[37] As an institution, slavery did not exist in Virginia in 1619. Slavery, as we know it today, evolved gradually beginning with customs rather than laws. To further shed light on how this institution evolved legally, from indentured servitude to life long servitude, the following laws and/or facts are given as well as other sources on 17th century servitude among Blacks in Virginia.[38] The enactment of these laws clearly outlines four distinct phases in their evolution and their impact on blacks.

New Towne in the 1660's by Keith Rocco
NPS COLO

Phase I - 1619 to 1638

During this phase, white and black servants were classified as indentured servants because the English colonies had not legalized slavery in its system of government. All indentured servants worked for a specified period as indicated in a contract between the servant and their master. Normally this was for a period of seven years and at the conclusion of the period of servitude, they would receive some recompense to aid them in starting anew. During this period, blacks were allowed to have many of the amenities offered to the white gentry such as Land Grants, white and black indentured servants, use of the court system, and firearms. However, in 1639 a change in the laws no longer required African Americans to carry arms and ammunition. During this period, the black population in Virginia increased from 23 in 1625 to approximately 300 by 1648.

Phase II- 1640-1660

As the black population increased so did the number of restrictions. After 1640, the general concept of "Slave for life" began to evolve. This became evident as the Virginia General Assembly started passing laws that can be seen as a deliberate attempt to disenfranchise all African Americans.

John Punch became the first documented "slave for life" in 1640. John and two white indentured servants planned and executed an escape to Maryland where they were captured. Following their capture, John was singled out to become a slave for life; the two white servants were flogged and returned to their employers to complete their indenture-ship that was extended for one year. "Custom" gradually became law during this period. An examination of the laws passed by the Virginia General Assembly during this period will clearly demonstrate the denigration of the rights of slaves and free blacks. During this phase, a clear line was drawn between the rights of whites, black slaves, Native Americans, and free blacks.

Phase III- 1660-1680

The laws passed during this phase further restricted the freedom of all blacks and legalized different treatment for blacks, Native Americans and indentured whites. With the passing of these laws, the prospect of lifetime slavery for blacks became a reality. These laws jeopardized blacks that had previously gained their freedom. They included clauses that allowed free blacks to be returned to slave and indentured status if they could not provide for themselves and pay applicable taxes. They also could be returned to slave status if they committed a major crime, especially if it was against a white Christian.

Phase IV- 1680 – 1705

In 1705, codified slave laws were adopted almost unanimously throughout the southern slave states. These laws legalized harsh punishment, to include death, if any free

Negro or slave raised his hand in defense against any white Christian. Blacks were not allowed to use the white courts and were subjected to stringent white rules administered by the local authorities. Dismemberment and flogging were common punishments for unruly slaves that ran away or openly defied the laws.

After 1705, piecemeal laws were put into use, as stopgap measures, to fill the void whenever a situation arose that were not covered by an existing law. Although the Virginia Assembly made many attempts to disenfranchise the Free African Americans and deprive them of their freedom and independence, they could do little to destroy their pride of being born free. They survived the long-range impact of the various laws and in some instances, profited from the existence of the law.

One of the families that prospered, because of these laws, was the Jones family in eastern Virginia. The Jones family, whose freedom was established in the early 1600's, was one of several free black families residing in the Virginia counties of York, James City, New Kent, Charles City, Hampton, Surry, Isle of Wight, Suffolk, Norfolk, and Gloucester. However, the Jones family in James City County shared in the establishment of one of the oldest, legally recognized, Free Black Settlements in the southern slave states.[39] This settlement was established at the "Hot Water Tract (Plantation)" in 1803 and is known today as Freedom Park, located near the City of Williamsburg, Virginia, in James City County, at the intersection of Longhill and Centerville Roads.

EVOLUTION OF VIRGINIA SLAVE LAWS

Some historians record the arrival of "20 and Odd" Blacks at Jamestown in late August of 1619 as the beginning of slavery in America. These Africans were allegedly sold/traded into servitude for supplies.

1630's Indications by surviving Wills, inventories, deeds and other documents are that, in some instances, it was considered "customary practice to hold some Negroes in a form of life service." It should be noted that by examining these documents it was also found that some blacks were able to hold on to their status of being indentured servants, thus, eventually gaining their freedom.

1639 All persons except Negroes and Indians are required to be with (carry) Arms and Ammunition.

1640 John Punch, a black runaway indentured Servant, became the first documented slave for life. Black women became taxable.

1662	Slavery became a recognized status in the statutory law of the colony. The Virginia General Assembly passed legislation defining the status of mulatto children. Children would have the same status as the mother. If the child were born of a slave, the child would be a slave. If the mother were free, the child would be born free.
1667	Prior to 1667, any black person that was baptized could be given their freedom. This was because it was not proper under British Law for a Christian to enslave a fellow Christian. Until the General Assembly outlawed it 1667, baptism could be the sole ground for a black slave to obtain his/her freedom.
1669	An Act was passed that allowed the "accidental" killing of slaves. If any slave resisted his master, the master was allowed to inflict physical punishment. If the slave died because of the punishment, the owner was not accountable. In 1670, a law was passed that prohibited free blacks and Native Americans from owning white "Christian" servants.
1680	An act was passed to prevent insurrections among slaves. Blacks could not congregate in large numbers for supposed funeral or feasts. Blacks must also obtain written authorization to

leave a plantation at any given time. They could not remain at another plantation longer than 4 hours.

1691 First act passed prohibiting intermarriage. The law provided for the banishment of any white person violating this law. No Negro or Mulatto may be set free by any person unless he pay for their transportation out of the colony within six months of being set free or forfeit ten pounds of sterling so that the churchwardens might have the Negro or Mulatto transported. A systematic plan was established to capture runaway slaves.

1692 Negroes must give up ownership of horses, cattle or pigs. Separate courts were established for the trial of slaves charged with a capital crime, thus depriving them of the right of a trial by jury.

1700's Slaves composed half of Virginia's unfree labor force.

1705 Slave laws were codified.

CHAPTER III

Education and Religion

The Bray School, 1760-1774

"In 1760, Virginia's first school for the education of slave children and free blacks officially opened in Williamsburg."[40] The "Associates of Dr. Bray", a charity closely tied to the Anglican Church and located in London, England, sponsored the School. Two local trustees, the rector of Bruton Parish Church and a prominent citizen, Mr. William Hunter, Editor of the Gazette, administered Williamsburg's school. The mistress of the school was a widowed white woman, Anne Wager. For fourteen years, she taught more than twenty-five students at a time to read the Bible, cipher, and learn the catechism of the Anglican Church."[41] Some members of the Jones family attended this school, and later became residents of the Hot Water Settlement.[42]

It should be noted that, during this period, public interest in education for slaves and free blacks was extremely rare.

Since the government made no provisions for the education of slaves and free blacks, all educational efforts were largely private actions initiated by white churches. The desire to educate slaves was non-existent and the sentiment against the education of free blacks was extremely strong. Southern whites generally believed that the education of free blacks would ultimately lead to them becoming discontented and developing ideas about willfully breaking the slave laws in an attempt to overthrow slavery. All of the southern states established laws prohibiting the education of free blacks. However, a surprisingly large number of them learned at least the fundamentals in spite of the barriers established by the white community.

My grandfather said that some of the children who had attended the Bray School were able to read and write and were referred to by many as "The first black teachers in Virginia". This is especially true of the Ashby and Jones children who taught members of their families to read, write and cipher (do math). He also said that with this introduction to education some free blacks were able to improve their reading and math skills beyond that of most whites in the area. The free blacks firmly believed that education would help them improve their condition in the community. According to my grandfather, the free blacks believed "Where opportunities did not exist, education would open the doors." My grandfather's comments are supported by John Hope Franklin in "From Slavery To Freedom", where he notes:

"Free Negroes in Virginia and North Carolina received private instruction from whites and other free Negroes, but very little in the schools".

During this period, the education and conversion of slaves to Christianity was a primary mission of Virginia's Baptist and Presbyterian Churches.[43] In the early 1800's the education of free Blacks and slaves was prohibited in Virginia, however, young students who had attended the Bray School continued to teach other free blacks in secret.

New Jerusalem

In the early and mid 1700s African-Americans were allowed to practice religion, but only as directed by the white populace.[44] They were required to attend church services along with their masters. During this period, they were not allowed to congregate for meetings of any type unless they had the approval and supervision of white overseers or masters. By 1760, Virginia's population grew to almost 300,000. Slaves and free blacks represented close to 40 percent of the total population. Many Anglican clergymen worked tirelessly to teach and convert the slaves to Christianity. Free African-Americans and African-American slaves were required to register with the parish vestry shortly after birth.[45] The requirement to register the birth of slaves was purely for economical reasons. All blacks above the age of sixteen became tithe-able and the Church collected the tithes (taxes). Whites became tithe-able at age eighteen.

The vestry records at Bruton Parrish Church show that blacks were included in its membership and received the services of the church. Although Negroes attended the church as parishioners and guests, they were allowed to sit only in the north gallery.[46] However, these restrictions on their assembly and meetings were often times bypassed. Because of the independence of the free blacks in the Williamsburg area, and their ability to move about freely, they were able to establish secret meeting places where religious services were held without the observation of white overseers.

This brings us to an era where secret meetings were held in various locations throughout James City County and neighboring counties. Thus, free blacks and slaves in James City County were able to establish their "New Jerusalem". The name, New Jerusalem, was a code name used for their secret meeting place near Jamestown where they held their religious services.[47] This secret hiding place or meeting place was located north of Green Spring Farm adjacent to the county road now referred to as "Brick Bat Road". The free black and slave communities nicknamed Brick Bat Road and called it "New Jerusalem Road". Initially, these religious services were held in this area without the knowledge of the slave owners.[48]

In an attempt to hide these meetings from whites in the area, blacks continued to attend church services along with their white masters. Due to the lengthy formality of the services and discriminating practices in the worship services, blacks longed for the day when they could worship openly as they pleased.

Liberation came as other denominations gained a foothold on American Soil and as the colonies became more and more distant in their relationship with England. This freedom came during the Baptists movement when Robert Carter, a wealthy white plantation owner, who owned more than 500 slaves, allowed blacks to worship as they pleased.[49] With the permission of their master(s), slaves built a Brush Harbor in 1776 at Robert Carter's green spring farm.[50] Although they were allowed to worship as they pleased, they were still required to have a white person present during their meetings, thus many of the blacks continued to meet secretly at New Jerusalem.

The number of blacks attending services increased rapidly in the area due to the building of the Brush Harbor at Carter's green spring farm. As a result, many of the blacks that lived and worked in Williamsburg, that had attended services at New Jerusalem, decided to move to a new and more accessible location east of Carter's farm. This new location was a lower area and was called "Raccoon Chase".[51]

Although there are no historical records that document its specific location, some local historians believe it to be on or near the Colonial Parkway near College Creek and the Gospel Spreading Church Farm. This area is located just north of the Colonial Parkway. In addition, they say that the Brush Harbor was moved two miles east of Jamestown. However, based on oral history, as told by my grandfather and others, a different location was used by the early Jones family church members.

According to my grandfather, the Brush Harbor was moved two miles east of its original location at Carter's green spring farm. This would place the Brush Harbor near Jerusalem Baptist Church. This area was known among the older blacks as "Coon Chase." This location is approximately two miles northeast of Jamestown and South of the Hot Water Tract.

From approximately 1763 to 1865 "New Jerusalem" was used routinely by free black and slave groups for religious services. Splinter groups formed several black churches in the area. Three of these splinter groups later formed the Chickahominy, New Zion and Zion Baptist churches. Today, there is a dilapidated building still standing at that location. The building is all that remains of the old "Jerusalem Baptist Church" that was built after the civil war at the site where the secret meetings were first held. Religious services were secretly held in this area prior to 1763.

The founders of this church were members of the Cannady, Howard, Jones, Williams, Richards, Smith, Jackson, Brown, Taylor and Wallace families, whose ancestors still live in the area. From this church, many of the Jones family later became members of the newer churches such as the Chickahominy Baptist Church, New Zion Baptist Church and Zion Baptist Church.

33

Chickahominy Baptist Church - Founded in 1865. Courtesy - L. Jones

New Zion Baptist - 1876-1902
Courtesy L. Jones

CHAPTER IV

Hot Water: An island of freedom in the middle of slavery

The story of Hot Water and its significance to the Jones family and the evolution of slavery in the United States has never been told. This effort represents the first attempt at elevating Hot Water to more than just a place where a bunch of freed African-Americans lived. Although Hot Water is significant to local, regional and national history, its story has been excluded from history.

Some of the early Land patents in the mid 1600 have referred to a tract of land identified in property boundaries as the "Hot Water Dividend" and the "Hot Water Tract". Originally, a large part of the Hot Water Tract belonged to Mr. Robert Wetherall. On May 15, 1652, Sir William Berkeley, the Royal Governor of Virginia, purchased 700 acres of the Hot Water Tract from Mr. Wetherall, and the remaining 300 acres of the tract from Mr. Richard Bell. The Hot Water Tract was located adjacent to and north of Green Springs Plantation, the primary residence of Governor Berkeley.[52] The geographical area occupied by Hot Water has been the site of many historical activities, some of which have been told when it related to the activities of the colonial founders and the major participants in the revolutionary and civil wars.

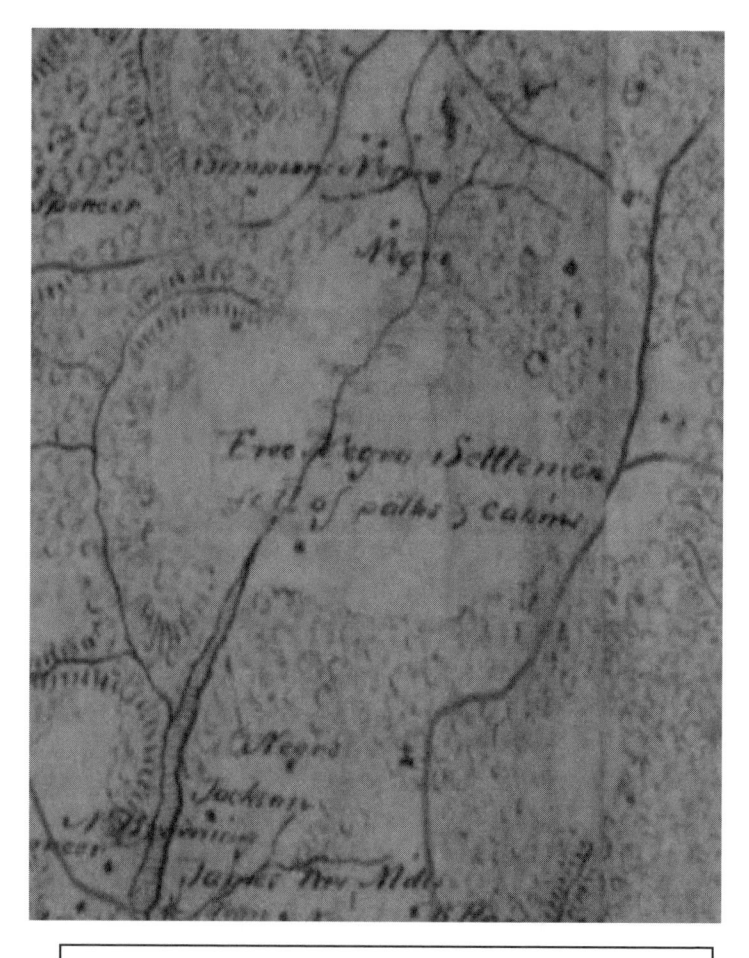

Hot Water Settlement Map By Gilmer, J. F., Confederate Cartographer and Engineer 1864 Courtesy U.S. Library of Congress PPD

Military battles were conducted in this area during the Indian uprisings in the 1600's, the Revolutionary War, and the Civil War. It also was part of the site of the battle at Spencer's Ordinary where colonial and French forces under the command of the Marquis De'Lafayette fought squirmishes against the British and Hessian forces.

Green Spring Plantation -Home of Virginia's Royal Governor Berkeley
~Benjamin Latrobe, 1770

In 1667, Governor Berkeley died and left his entire Virginia Estate to his wife, Lady Frances. In 1679, she acquired an additional 285 acres east of the Hot Water Tract. This new acquisition was soon incorporated as part of the Hot Water Tract and extended across the old Jamestown Road (State Road 614/Centerville Road) and north of old Williamsburg Road (Known today as Long Hill Road).[53]

With the approval of her family, Lady Frances married Phillip Ludwell I, a wealthy planter. For some unknown reason their marriage failed to produce a viable heir, therefore upon their deaths Phillip Ludwell I's son, Phillip Ludwell II, inherited their land holdings. Through this twist of fate, the Ludwell and Berkeley estates became one of the largest estates in Virginia. It extended from east of the Chickahominy River to West of College Creek. After his death in 1727 there was a succession of heirs until William Ludwell Lee, his great grandson, and founder of the Free Black Settlement at Hot Water, inherited the properties.

In the late 1700's, world opinion and events concerning slavery began to affect the American system of slavery. As the natural rights theories of John Locke, a renowned British Philosopher, were introduced into the world community, a climate of change began to occur in countries such as England and France. According to John Locke's theories, "All men are created equal and possessed with certain inalienable rights that no one should be able to take from them. He stated that chief among these rights are the right to pursue, health, life, liberty and possessions".

Over a short period of time Locke's theories lead to a consensus in Europe, and the Europeans, especially France and England, gradually began to feel that slavery should be abolished and initiated a series of actions to eliminate slavery in areas where they were in control. These same thoughts also permeated American thinking and gave new life to the abolitionist movement in America. As white Americans began to think about their demands for freedom from England, they had to consider the enslavement of Africans in America. The Americans, with good conscience, could not use Locke's theories as the basis for rebellion against England and at the same time continues their practice of slavery. Some of the more enlightened Americans realized that the demise of slavery in America was near at hand and began to take positive actions to prepare for this eventuality.

Other events affecting the issue of slavery in America were the increase in the number of slave uprisings in America, South America, Mexico, and the Caribbean. Another factor affecting slavery in America was the large number of runaway slaves. According to the book "History Lessons", by Dana Lindaman and Kyle Ward, more than 200,000 runaway slaves from the southern states had found sanctuary in Louisiana under the French "Statute of Free Men".

Because of these world events, some of the Slave Owners in America began the voluntary emancipation of their slaves. Among these were Robert Carter, William Norvell and William Ludwell-Lee, three of the wealthiest landowners in James City County, Virginia, who shocked the entire south when they introduced the idea that "To retain Negroes in Slavery is contrary to the true principles of Religion and Justice". With this thought, they began setting goals and timelines for the release of their slaves. They all made provisions in their wills for the release of their slaves upon their death. Ironically, these gentlemen died within a few short years of each other.

William Ludwell-Lee set aside a portion of the Hot Water Tract as a home-site for his newly released slaves and made provision in his will to insure their survival. However, Robert Carter, due to his large holdings, more than 500 slaves and 18 plantations in Virginia, was not able to do the same thing for his slaves. However, when you research the original residents of Hot Water, the family name Carter becomes very prominent. This may indicate that some of Robert Carter's slaves settled at Hot Water. William Norvell started releasing his slaves during the early 1790's.

William Ludwell-Lee specified in his will that his slaves over eighteen years old would be freed on January 1st, one year after his death. His will was prepared on July 14, 1802 and he died January 24, 1803. His early demise at the tender age of twenty-seven did not come as a surprise as he had been ill for some time. He was single at the time of his death and had no heirs other than his two sisters, to whom he left most of his real and personal estate. His will stated that his executors were to set aside a portion of the Hot Water tract for his freed slaves to live and work.[54]

He specified that they were to have comfortable houses built at the expense of his estate; they were to receive a year's supply of corn and allowed to live on the land for ten years "free of any charge". Some individuals were to receive farming instruments and tools pertaining to their tradecraft. He also indicated that all slaves younger than eighteen were to be sent to a state north of the Potomac River to be educated at the expense of his estate.[55] However, there are no known records or concrete proof that the younger slaves were sent out of the state to be educated.

William Ludwell-Lee's last Will & Testament {extract} containing a provision for the emancipation of slaves at his Hot Water lands.
County Records Alexandria, VA

The timing of Lee's will and his demise proved crucial to his slaves' being able to stay in Virginia, because within three years after his death the State General Assembly passed legislation that required all newly emancipated slaves to leave the state. Because his Will and subsequent death preceded the new legislation, the provisions of his will were "Grandfathered" (made retroactive) and applied to his slaves. Therefore, his slaves that were released after his death were allowed to remain in the state and settle in Hot Water.

Prior to the establishment of Hot Water as a sanctuary for the slaves freed by William Ludwell Lee, free blacks, mulattoes, and other indentured servants were already working and living on the Hot Water Tract. These groups had been allowed to work at the Hot Water Tract as sharecroppers. They worked small patches of land and received a portion of the crops for their own personal use.[56]

Some of these free African Americans ventured into the world of entrepreneurship by selling a part of their crops at a local market frequented by other free blacks and white indentured servants, while others were able to purchase property and servants. This market was located on a dirt road located west of the Hot Water Boundary. The site for this market would later become the location for a store operated by Coleman and Gracie Richardson in the early 1900's.[57] Normally the slaves/servants purchased by the free blacks were their spouses, children and other relatives that were in bondage.[58]

People of Hot Water

Now that we have properly addressed the Hot Water tract, it is time for us to meet the people of Hot Water. First, we will meet the Joneses then some of the slaves that gained their freedom because of William Ludwell Lee's humanitarian effort. Much of the following information was derived from James City County personal property tax documents, wills, family documents, oral history from family members and materials researched by other local historians.

According to an analysis of the available Personal Property Tax Rolls compiled in 1802 and 1804, it would appear that at least fourteen slaves, eleven men and three women, were released in 1804. They were identified as Aaron, John Jackson, Charles Carter, Guy, Humphrey Howard (Harrod or possibly Harwood), Jiles (William Giles), the Lee brothers (Henry, Isaac and James), Michael Nelson and John Ralph.[59] The three women were Beulah, Bessie and Mary. The majority of this group settled in the southern most part of Hot Water in an area they had nicknamed "New Jerusalem".[60] Several of their descendants live in this area today. Brick Bat Road, Centerville Road and the southern most part of Jolly Pond Road encompasses the area.

Subsequently, additional slaves were freed as they became of age as specified in William Ludwell-Lee's will. For the most part, these slaves lived in the center and eastern part of the area known today as Hot Water and Freedom Park. Among these were the Brown, Carter, Crawley,

Giles, Griffin, Harris, Howard, Jackson, Johnson, Lee, Richardson, Taylor, and Wallace (Wallis) families. Many of these families successfully transitioned from Slave to Free and their descendents have led successful lives in the community that now surrounds Hot Water.

In addition to the freed slaves, there were a sizeable number of Free Black families already living in Hot Water. Many of these Free Black families had been working as indentured servants and subsistence farmers. These Free Blacks represented more than two thirds of the families living in Hot Water between 1834 and 1863. Today they can be recognized by the surnames ... Cannaday, Cox, Cumber, Cumbo, Harrod, Jones, Lightfoot, Mason, Moore, Morris, Roberts, Tyler, and Wallace.

Between 1803 and 1810, there were two free black communities in James City County. One was at Weir Creek and the other was at the Hot Water Tract. Although there were two free black settlements in the county, most of the inhabitants at both locations were related.

Based on research it would appear that the settlement at Weir creek was established in a piecemeal fashion while the Hot Water settlement was more structured and planned. Weir Creek was home to the Ashlock, Bervine, Collier, Hodson, Nelson, and Taylor families. Later, the Joneses, Tyler and other families would move into the area. These families moved back and forth across ware Creek, the Boundary between James City County and New Kent County. This movement was necessary for employment purposes.[61] According to county tax rolls and other county records, the newly freed blacks were employed in a variety of jobs.

Most of the heads of household, in both settlements, were men and lived with their wives and children, but some shared their homes with members of their extended family, orphaned children and others who may not have been related. Contrary to what some historians have incorrectly reported, black families had extremely strong bonds and the black male was the dominant figure in the household.

(The next chapter visits some of the Freedmen and newly freed slaves that lived in Hot Water at the same time as my great, great, grandfather as revealed through a collection of historical documents, county records and oral history.)

CHAPTER V

The Jones Family and Oral Histories

George A. Jones and his story about the beginning of the Jones family in America and the Hot Water Tract as told to the Author.

George A. Jones, age 103, (1870-1973)
Courtesy - L. Jones

My Grandfather, George A. Jones, was born in 1870 and died in 1973. His wife, Mary, preceded him in death. Grandpa worked as a farmer, Longshoreman, and railroad worker. He retired from the railroad prior to my birth. According to him, he and several of his ancestors supervised farm production for the college of William and Mary located in Williamsburg, Virginia.

Since Grandpa George knew his grandfather, James, who was born in 1803 and lived in the Hot Water Area, he was able to provide me with a wealth of first hand information about Hot Water and its early residents. His grandfather James died in 1891. James and Sarah Collier Jones, his Grandparents, are listed in the James City County Personal Property Tax List for 1834 and in the 1850 Census as Freedmen.

In addition, he told me about things that his family and other free blacks did during the civil war as told to him by his parents, John and Margaret Jones.

Other oral history resources were my Cousin Lula Howard Lattimore (1908-2005), Cousin Bessie Tabb (1907-2003), Aunt Hazel Byrd (95 years old), Grand Uncle Andrew Jones (1887-1977), Uncle John Jones (93 years old) and Uncle William Jones (91 years old), all of whom lived in or adjacent to Hot Water as young children.

I remember walking with my grandfather, George, along the area in James City County called Hot Water, now known as Freedom Park, where he would share the stories his grandfather, James Jones, had told him. He was very proud that his ancestors had begun life in this country as indentured servants, although forty years later blacks were routinely classified as slaves.

He would say, "When I was a little boy about your age, growing up in Hot Water, my granddaddy and daddy would take my brothers and me to different parts of the county and would tell us the same history that I am telling you. Whenever they started telling the story, I would notice something that I had missed before. I am telling you this because the more times you hear the story the more you will remember when you get old like me."

My grandfather and father said that the Jones' family history might have started in America with the arrival of the first Africans at Jamestown in 1619. According to them, our first black ancestors in America arrived aboard a Dutch ship from the Caribbean. Although they were traded for supplies, it is believed that they were classified as indentured servants rather than as slaves. They also told me that, as far as they knew, the Jones men had never been emotionally or physically enslaved. In fact, my granddaddy used to say, "There are only three things in this world that you can't control, and they are the time and place of your birth and the time of your death. Everything else is manageable."

It was during this time and much later that I decided to find out more information and historical data that my grandfather would have found if he had had the resources and opportunity. The story continues from oral and written historical sources.

Our family's story began in America when one of our African ancestors arrived in America from the Caribbean and became intimately involved with a white female indentured servant. They had several children and all of their offspring were classified as mulattoes (Various court and church records, and the Virginia Census for 1850 and 1880).

Years later, another white indentured servant, identified in records as Elizabeth Jones, became a member of our family. Elizabeth and her sister, Mary, arrived in America from London, England. Because of their religious beliefs, which were at odds with the Anglican Church, Elizabeth and Mary had been separated from their families in England and sentenced to go to prison or to the new colony in Virginia as indentured servants. They chose to come to Virginia. At that time, they were placed in New Gate Prison, London, England, until they could be shipped to the colonies.

After landing on the York River, they traveled by foot with a group of men to the Powhatan District (Known today as James City County). Based on the records that Elizabeth was white and her Common-Law spouse was John Jones, a free-mulatto, their children were classified as mulattoes. In addition, these children became free people because the status of children was based on the status of their mother, as prescribed by colonial law. Because they were born of free white mothers, they were sometimes called " issue free Negroes."

Shortly after Elizabeth and Mary were freed, (completed their indenture), they sent for other family members. According to my grandfather, Emmanuel Jones, their brother, arrived in America aboard the ship Pretty Patsie. Along with him were his three sons, Thomas, William, and John. They landed in Maryland and traveled by horseback and wagon to James City County where they settled down and began their new life. Our family began to grow and thrive shortly after these three brothers arrived. According to family folklore, and as supported by historical documents found in records at Colonial Williamsburg, their father, Emanuel, became seriously ill and had to return to England. His sons worked as sharecroppers and took possession of his lands, which had been obtained from the Ludwell-Lee Family. The land previously was owned by the Royal Governor, Sir William Berkeley, and was part of the Berkeley Plantation.

Due to a shortage of eligible females, the three brothers married Indian women believed to be from the Mattaponi, Pamunkey or Chickahominy tribes. Because they married Indian women, their marriages were not recorded in court records. According to my grandfather, their marriages were referred to as "Coming together". Their children were classified as Mulattos and certified as being free people.

When William Ludwell-Lee, a wealthy James City County Plantation owner, died in 1803, a part of his land, known as the "Hot Water Tract" was set a side for some of his slaves who were freed the year following his death.

Lady Frances Berkeley, Museum of Early Southern Decorative Arts By Permission

Shortly thereafter, members of the Jones Family began to marry the former slaves. This led to the infusion of Mulattos, American Indians and African-American slaves in Hot Water. The Jones Family have been documented in historical records as one of the oldest free black families in the United States and one of the few that can document its infusion with Whites and American Indians during this period.

As free black people the Jones family was able to spread out and live all along the east coast (North Carolina, South

Carolina, Virginia, and Maryland) during the 1600's, 1700's, and 1800's. Several family members served in the Revolutionary War, war of 1812, Civil War and the Spanish American War. There are documented government service records for several of these ancestors.[62]

Family members performed jury duty in the late 1800's, and owned small stores and other businesses in James City and York County. Other family members worked as Blacksmiths, Woodsmen, Silversmiths, Farmers, Carpenters, Shoemakers, Surveyors, Longshoreman, Waggoner, Steveadores and Carriage Men.[63] Locally, the Jones family owned several pieces of property in Hot Water and in adjacent areas such as Centerville, Chickahominy, Shields Point, and Black Stump.[64] However, some of their records of ownership were destroyed in a fire during the civil war. Nevertheless, a few of them were able to retain their property because they had certified "Back Pocket Deeds" (Copies of deeds left at home).

Life for the Joneses was slightly different from that of most African Americans because they were designated as mulattoes and classified as free people. Thus, they were relatively free to travel around Williamsburg, James City County, York County and Charles City where they were known by most of the white people they came into contact. For the most part, travel outside of these areas was limited to the male family members.[65]

The female members normally restricted their travel to taking produce and homemade products to the local markets in Williamsburg and James City County or to the homes of whites where they were employed as laundresses, cooks, housekeepers and childcare givers. Female members of the family rarely traveled outside of these areas, unless it was part of a family relocation. Also, due to the turmoil in relations between free-whites, indentured servants, free-blacks and slave hires, the women were not allowed to travel alone.[66]

During their travels outside the immediate area of Williamsburg and James City County, family members were required to have, in their possession, some form of documentation that verified that they were free people. Even with this documentation, they had to be extremely careful when traveling because there was always a chance that they would encounter a group of illiterate "Peterrollers" (white men conducting slave patrols) bent on kidnapping and selling them into slavery in the Deep South.

Some of the Jones men traveled outside of the area on a frequent basis to all parts of Virginia and North Carolina seeking work and visiting family members. Sometimes they drove wagonloads of goods to places like Norfolk, Richmond and Petersburg, Virginia. They also transported goods into various parts of North Carolina. When they went into North Carolina, they had to have in their possession a "special pass" or certificate signed by a justice of the peace stating that they were free men. Although they were free, they sometimes traveled in the company of a white business owner. When traveling without a white person present, a maximum of three men would travel together to preclude the white people they encountered from being overly afraid of a contingent of blacks. Occasionally one of them would "pass for white" to make their trips easier.

One story that persists in our family history is about the time that my great, great, grandfather, James and his brother, William, were hauling a wagonload of dry goods from Williamsburg to a store in Amelia County, Virginia. Shortly after they passed Richmond, Virginia, it started to rain very heavily. They continued on their way until they encountered a part of the road that had washed away. While attempting to go around the washed out section of the road a wheel on the wagon broke and they were unable to repair it. They started walking towards the nearest settlement to get help. As nightfall began to set in, they became concerned about the curfew that was established for free blacks and slaves. Soon they saw a large house in the distance and began to develop a plan to get them out of the weather. Because William had a very light complexion, gray eyes and was very articulate, they decided that he would pretend to be a white trader and James would pretend to be his slave.

William bravely walked up on the front porch and knocked on the door while James nervously stood out in the rain. When the white man who lived in the house came to the door, William quickly said to him, "My boy and I were taking a load of dry goods to the store over in Amelia, but the wheel on my wagon broke and we couldn't fix it. Do you have some tools that we can borrow?" The white man took a long, close look at William and said, "Come on in, you must be soaked." The white man then said to William, "Sir! As you see, we are just now sitting down for dinner. If you want, you can clean up and have dinner with us". William thanked him and quickly went over to the washbasin, cleaned his face and hands and sat down at the table. The white man walked over to the door and yelled outside to James saying, "Boy, you go to the back and tell the cook to give you something to eat." After dinner, the man told William that he could stay the night and that in the morning he could use his tools and some wood to fix the wagon. That night William slept in the house and James slept out in the barn. The next morning they fixed the wagon and continued on their way to Amelia County. They did this fully realizing that if caught "passing" for white they could be immediately enslaved or killed.

Although the Joneses were classified as mulattoes, they still experienced many of the problems faced by the slave population when dealing with the whites. Additionally, they were always suspected by the white gentry of creating a resistance to slavery among the slaves they encountered. In addition, because they were able to accumulate modest wealth and property, many of the poor white population despised them and did all sorts of things to intimidate them and undermine their status.

Because they were more literate than some of the whites in the county, and some of the whites they met while traveling, they had to pretend to be illiterate, or as my granddaddy would say "Negro Down". They had to do this because if there was one thing a southern white man could not tolerate it was an educated black man.

They were subjected to many unpleasantries and new restrictions imposed by the local authorities and the Virginia General Assembly immediately following reports of slave uprisings in nearby areas. When these events took place, the Joneses and other free-blacks were denied most of the basics rights originally given them.

As a very young boy, I spent a lot of time with my grandfather, George, fishing, hunting and riding around on a horse drawn wagon. We would ride around the county and he would tell me stories about the origin of the Jones family, people in the community and the untold black history of the area. Since my grandfather lived with us, he and I formed a very close bond. He taught me how to have respect for our culture and who I was as a person. Grandpa was an excellent judge of character and he revealed to me many of the ways he used to analyze people.

Often, he said, "Grandson, I am going to teach you things about life that will guarantee your success as a man." One of the most important things he taught me was how to gain knowledge and how to build on that knowledge by applying common sense. I strongly believe that because of his influence I was able to achieve excellent grades in school and, subsequently, obtain a scholarship that enabled me to get a college education.

When we took our "little trips" as he called them, he would point out old home sites where free blacks had lived, plantation sites, historical battlefields, Indian campsites, old slave quarters, natural water springs, old graveyards and destroyed mansions.

One area he liked to talk about was Hot Water and its history as a free black settlement. According to his father and grandfather, Hot Water was the "perfect place" for a free black settlement. It offered fresh water from three natural springs, well-fertilized soil for planting crops, wild game and waterfowl, timber for the building of log cabins and seclusion from the rest of the community in James City County. There were many log cabins and a few Shanties built in Hot Water but they were all substantial when compared with the homes of white indentured servants and poor whites.

58

Tyler House – Built in Hot Water circa. 1840. Courtesy - L. Jones

Grandpa told me that the men that lived in Hot Water built the houses. A few of them would get together and build a house by cutting down trees in the area and hewing out the timber to make the pieces for the ceilings and the walls. They also would build lofts in the log cabins so they could be used for sleeping. Usually the children would sleep up in the lofts. The boys would sleep in one loft and the girls in the other. The parents usually had a bedroom downstairs. Sometimes they would build small extensions along the side of the house for storage and for use as additional sleeping space as the family grew in size.

Hot Water as it would have appeared, about 1850 ~Library of Congress, P&P

Some of the other people living in Hot Water had similar houses, but the majority of the people lived in homes that were nothing more than small wood frame clapboard homes. The small framed clapboard houses were very simple and consisted of three or four small rooms with simple partitions or blankets hung on a rail to separate the bedrooms from the remainder of the house.

Typical Hot Water Home (1803-1830)
built on site At Freedom Park 2007
Courtesy - L. Jones

They would fill the cracks with mud, clay from the swamp, and old rags. The women would take flour and paper to make paper-mache sheets to plaster the walls. This made the houses nice and warm during the winter because it kept the cold air out. In addition, during the summer, when it was hot, the paper-mache coverings could be removed and stored to allow cool air to enter the house through the cracks in the walls. The people who lived in them would sometimes paint the walls.

Typical Frame Home 1850-1865 built on site at Hot Water 2007
Courtesy - L. Jones

Grandpa told me that there were two sites in Hot Water where old mansions used to be. He also told me that the British destroyed the mansions during the revolutionary war and that most of the remnants of the buildings were carried away by white farmers and free blacks.

While riding around he would some times give me a glimpse of his humor by telling little stories about the people he met. There was one white man in particular that I will never forget. We would see him quite often as we rode around in the wagon and he would always call my grandfather "Uncle George". I could tell by my grandfather's disposition that the man's greeting bothered him. One day, grandpa said to me, "If I see that man today, I am going to tell him a thing or two about calling me Uncle George". About an hour later, we saw the man and he gave his usual greeting. Immediately my grandfather asked him "Why do you always call me Uncle George?" The man's reply was, "I call you that out of respect for your age". Grandpa quickly replied, "I don't like you calling me Uncle George because I am not related to you, but if you insist on calling me something out of respect, try calling me Daddy or Mr. Jones." From that point on the man called grandpa "Mr. Jones".

When he talked about the people in general, he usually did it in a non-descript manner. However, when he talked about white people he would use stories or short allegories such as "Boy, remember that even if you are treated badly by some of the white people you meet, they are not all bad. However, in this area finding a good one is like looking under rocks for a bug. If you turn over enough rocks eventually you will find one, and the one you find will be a friend for life". He also had a saying about people visiting him at his home. He would always say to his friends, "If you are coming to visit make sure you come after lunch and leave before dinner".

When the Hot Water Settlement was first formed in 1803, his ancestors were already working there as freemen for more than 100 years. I was told that some of the family worked as sharecroppers for the Lee family and Governor Berkeley for as long as my family could remember. Others worked in different jobs such as Fishermen, woodsmen, Craftsmen, blacksmiths, sharecroppers and independent farmers on their own land. Some were bootleggers and others were just outright scoundrels. However, that is another story by itself.

My grandfather told me that his father, John T. Jones was born in 1842, and that our family surname, Jones, was adopted in the 1600's after the first family members were baptized and became Christians. They chose the name Jones because they had worked for Captain Matthew Jones as indentured servants. Captain Matthew Jones' house is located at present day Fort Eustis, Virginia.

Both of his parents talked about how some of their ancestors had worked their own farms and how others worked in different jobs. They said that during the old days, about a third of the black people were free and this made the white people nervous.

Captain Matthew Jones House - Fort Eustis, Newport News, Virginia
Courtesy - L. Jones

They would talk about the great fear among the whites because there were so many free blacks in the area, especially after the uprising that was led by Nat Turner over in South Hampton County. After the slave revolts down south and Nat Turner's rebellion, the State of Virginia passed legislation that barred all black people, to include free blacks, mulattoes and Indians, from owning dogs and guns, unless they were given to them by a white person, had a written authorization from a prominent white land-owner or legal authority, to possess and use them.

Nevertheless, that did not work in Hot Water. Although the law said that this rule also applied to all free blacks, most of the free black men kept their guns and would hide them whenever the sheriff or his deputies came into the area. At night, they would use their guns to go raccoon hunting.

According to my grandfather, "All of this stuff started happening in the late 1830's". Until that time, white men rarely came into Hot Water after it was set-a-side for freed slaves to build homes and farm. Grandpa said that the best thing that ever happened in this area was when the Lee Family freed their slaves and let them come to live in Hot Water. This allowed the former slaves and the free blacks to mingle and have children that also became free men.

Sometimes the newly freed slaves would obtain loans to buy the freedom of their spouses and children if they were still enslaved. They would then "work off" the loan, but would keep their spouses and children listed as their slaves. They did this because all newly freed slaves were required to leave the state or be re-enslaved.

He said that the only time that his father and grandfather could remember a large group of white men coming into Hot Water was after Nat Turners rebellion over in South Hampton County in 1831 and during the civil war. They said that after Nat Turner's rebellion, white people in Williamsburg and the surrounding counties took extra precautions to stop any chance of an uprising in this area. All slaves that were hired out had to return to their owner's home and were not allowed to go anywhere, unless an armed white man escorted them. Free blacks living in the city were told to stay at home under penalty of death if they failed to comply. Black sailors coming into the different ports along the James and York Rivers were placed in jail while their ships or boats were docked. The free blacks living in Hot Water were told not to leave the immediate area surrounding their homes. All roads leading into Hot Water were barricaded and guarded by armed white men. In addition, some of the local militia was called up and given different security duties to enforce the movement restriction orders. Random patrols by armed white men were conducted in Hot Water for about Two months.

The next time a large group of white men came into Hot Water was during the Civil War when a group of southern soldiers came into Hot Water. They said that the confederates came into the area and tried to get the free black men to fight with them and act as spies whenever the Yankees were in the area. Some of the men agreed to help just to appease the Confederate soldiers. Later in the war, the Union and Confederate soldiers fought a "good size battle" in Hot Water and War Hill, which was located on the eastern side of Centerville Road.

Instead, they helped the North by sending them drawings that showed where the confederates were camping and how many of them were at each location. Some of them acted as outriders for the North and reported the movement of the confederate soldiers. What the confederates did not realize was the fact that some free black men from Hot Water and some runaway slaves from nearby plantations had already enlisted in the Union Army. My father told me that he knew many of the black men from James City County that joined the Union forces because he was one of them.

When the North started recruiting black soldiers in Norfolk, Hampton and York County, several of the young black men from Hot Water and James City County sneaked away and joined the all black units. According to my father, he was one of those young men. He volunteered for the 2nd U.S. Cavalry (Colored Troops) after it was formed at Fort Monroe, Hampton, Virginia. The 1st and 2nd U.S. Calvary units later moved to Williamsburg and recruited more of the young black men that could ride a horse and shoot. They were camped near Jamestown where they were trained by white officers and black sergeants. He told me that they were issued used military equipment and oftentimes were short on needed supplies. In many instances, they had to forage.

After completing their training, they were used to defend Jamestown against Confederate forces and conduct patrols along a front that extended from New Kent to Richmond, and as far south as Petersburg and parts of North Carolina. Black soldiers from Hot Water, and other parts of the county, also fought in battles against the confederacy in many other Virginia locations.

The defense of Jamestown was very important to the north because it was the closest Union military post to Richmond, the Confederate Capitol, and it was in a location where Union forces could protect the Union Navy that it was building up in Hampton Roads. According to my father, Jamestown became a safe haven for runaway slaves who were trying to escape to the northern states. Sometimes the Union Navy would either enlist their services as laborers or take them to Northern Ports where they could reestablish themselves.

US Colored Calvary Troops, 1865
U.S. CIVIL WAR - Library of Congress

His father told him that his unit and several other black units fought in major battles throughout North Carolina and Virginia, especially around Richmond, Petersburg, and up in the Shenandoah mountains. He said that despite the fact that they were poorly equipped with old weapons, inferior equipment, and were always short on supplies and medical aid, they decisively won every battle they had against Confederate forces.

He also said that the white units were paid almost twice as much as they were paid and in some white units, the enlistees were paid more than black sergeants were paid. Although their white officers and the white units that they fought alongside discriminated against them, they took pride in what they were doing and served with valor and distinction.

John T. Jones (First_Last)	
Regiment Name 2 U.S. Col'd Cav.	
Side Union	
Company L	
Soldier's Rank_In Pvt.	
Soldier's Rank_Out Pvt.	
Alternate Name John F./Jones	
Notes	
Film Number M589 roll 49	

African American Civil War Memorial

Displayed as: John T. Jones ★

Plaque Number: A-4

(This plaque and the following highlighted regimental information are from the African American Civil War Memorial in Washington, D.C.)

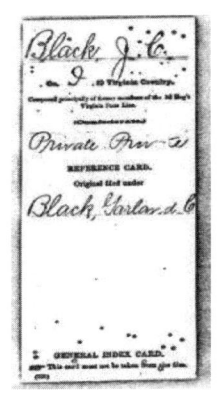

2nd Regiment Cavalry (Colored)

Organized at Fort Monroe, Va., December 22, 1863. Attached to Fort Monroe, Va., Dept. of Virginia and North Carolina, to April 1864. Unattached Williams-

burg, Va., Dept. of Virginia and North Carolina, to June 1864. 2nd Brigade, 3rd Division, 18th Corps, Army of the James, to August 1864. Unattached 3rd Division, 18th Corps, to December 1864. Unattached 25th Corps, Dept. of Virginia, to May 1865. Cavalry Brigade, 25th Corps, Dept. of Virginia and Dept. of Texas, to February 1866.

SERVICE. --Duty at Fort Monroe, Portsmouth and Williamsburg, Va., until May 1864. Demonstration on Portsmouth March 4-5. Action near Suffolk, Virginia, on March 10. Reconnaissance from Portsmouth to the Blackwater April 13-15. Butler's operations on the south side of James River and against Petersburg and Richmond May 4-28. Capture of Bermuda Hundred and City Point May 5. SwiftCreek May 8-10. Operations against Fort Darling May 10-16. Action at Drury's Bluff on May 10-13-14-15 and 16. Near Drury's Bluff May 20. Duty in trenches at Bermuda Hundred until June 13. Point of Rocks June 10. Richmond Campaign June 13-July 31. Baylor's Farm June 15. Assaults on Petersburg June 16-19. Siege of Petersburg and Richmond June 16, 1864, to February 18, 1865. Duty before Petersburg until July 1864. Moved to Deep Bottom July 25. Action at Deep Bottom July 27-28. Strawberry Plains, Deep Bottom, August 14-18. Actions at Deep Bottom September 2 and 6. Chaffin's Farm September 29-30. Darbytown Road October 7. Battle of Fair Oaks, Darbytown Road October 27-28. Near Richmond October 28-29. Duty in trenches north of James River until February 1865. Ordered to Norfolk February 18. Duty

in District of Eastern Virginia at Norfolk, Suffolk, etc., until May. Ordered to City Point, Va.; thence sailed for Texas June 10. Duty on the Rio Grande and at various points in Texas until February 1866. Mustered out February 12, 1866.

After the civil war, he returned home, married my mother and began raising our family. When he first returned to James City County, he worked as a subsistence farmer for some of the white landowners until he was able to obtain his own land in Hot Water. In addition, when I was a little boy, I remember him working on a farm that was owned by the College of William and Mary. I remember this because we would live there during the planting and harvesting times. At other times, we lived on our land in Hot Water.

When his father was not farming, he worked with some of the other black men and my uncles cutting wood. Like most men in Hot Water, his Daddy and Uncles all owned either a horse or an Ox. His Daddy had two horses, two mules, two oxen, three milk cows, a Farm Wagon and a Carriage. He also had several pigs and a chicken coup.

One of his horses was wild when he purchased him and no one could ride him. His name was 'Trixie' and he was the meanest horse I had ever seen. Trixie would start bucking as soon as a rider was on his back and after the rider was thrown off his back, he would try to kick or bite the rider. When daddy first purchased him, some of my uncles tried to 'break' him but he was too mean. They tried unsuccessfully for about two weeks. Daddy told them that they were wasting their time and that he would break Trixie within three days. They asked him how was he going to do that and he told them that it was a secret. He stuck to his words with them, but he told me that he was going to use an old Indian trick that he had learned while he was in Texas. He kept Trixie away from water for two days and did not give him anything to drink. On the third day, he took him to the pond and walked him out into the water until it reached the horse's sides. While the horse was drinking water, daddy got on his back and just sat there. When the horse was through drinking he tried to 'buck', but the water and mud on the bottom would not allow him. Daddy walked him around in the deep water for about thirty minutes and then rode him out of the pond. From that time on, Daddy was the only one who could ride Trixie.

Daddy also had a logging Wagon. It had two wheels and tilted down in the back when the horses backed up. This made it easy for the men to load the trees on the wagon and take them to the Sawmill. The men also would hand cut railroad-ties and sell them to the railroad and the Sawmill.

One of their biggest customers for cut timber was Mr. Samuel Harris. He was the owner of a large store in Williamsburg named Harris' Cheap Store, and was considered by many to be the richest black man in the state of Virginia. He and his wife had originally come from Richmond, Virginia. Both white and black families shopped at his store. When I was a young man, my wife and I shopped there. In fact, my cousin Sarah Howard worked for him at his home. Sarah married Henry Pierce who worked as a clerk at Sam Harris' store. Mr. Harris also owned several other businesses in the Williamsburg area.

Sarah Jones Baker (1868-1955)
Hot Water Resident, Seamstress and Butcher Shop Owner - Williamsburg, Virginia   Courtesy - L. Jones

74

Clarence Jones, Hot Water Resident, Hauling logs on a Two-wheel Wagon in Hot Water   Courtesy - L. Jones

Uncle William "Big Bill Jones" operated a Sawmill in Hot Water and was the main local provider of wood products to Sam Harris. Initially, Uncle Bill rented the Sawmill from an old white man whose name I cannot remember.

The Sawmill was located near old Hot Water road, about a half-mile from the Cemetery near Uncle Bill's house. My Uncle Wilmore Jones was Uncle Bill's brother. Uncle Wilmore supervised the cutters and logging crews in the area. They knew that there were some historic home sites and graveyards in the area and they tried their best not to destroy them with their logging operations.

They would cut timber and trim it out for building houses and other buildings. When they cut the rafters and some of the other parts they would match them up by cutting numbers and letters from the alphabet on the pieces where they joined. They said that when they did this it made it easier for them to put the rafters and other heavy boards together. Because almost all wood products were cut with hand tools, each cut was different and they had to match the pieces to get a snug fit.

Years later, my brother Andrew purchased the Sawmill and continued logging and mill operations until about 1937. Let me tell you, Andrew Jones was one man you did not want to aggravate. He was an expert shot with a pistol and a rifle. When we were growing up all the Jones men were known to be great Horsemen and expert riflemen. However, Andrew took it a bit further. When he was about 11, he started going from house to house looking for work so he could earn money to by bullets.

After buying his ammunition, he would take daddy's pistol and rifle down to the creek and practice shooting at bottles and cattail bunches in the marsh. By the time he was 14, he was one of the best shots in the county. He would lay the bottles down on their side and turn the mouth of the bottles towards him. Then he would walk off a distance of about fifty feet, kneel down with the rifle, take aim and shoot through the neck of the bottle blowing the bottoms out. At other times, he would throw five bottles into the air at the same time and break them with the pistol before they hit the ground.

Andrew Jones (1886-1977)
Entrepreneur Hot Water
Courtesy - L. Jones

Andrew was an astute businessperson as indicated by his purchase of the Sawmill. He also owned a grocery store, Blacksmith shop, and laundry about a half mile south of the intersection of Jolly Pond Road and Centerville Road. He managed the garage, laundry and grocery store while our brother Wilmore managed the Sawmill. His businesses were located on the south side of Ernest Jones' house. In 1941, Andrew converted his Blacksmith shop into a garage. He sold his businesses and retired in 1946. He also was a short-term actor for Colonial Williamsburg where he played the roll of a white farmer in a film that was shown to tourists at the Visitor Center.

One thing that the family and others remember about him was his ability to persuade people to accept his ideas. As an example, he had a policy of paying his employees half of their pay on Friday and the balance on Monday. When the employees asked him why he was doing it, he simply said, "If I pay you all of your money on Friday you will spend all of it drinking and having a good time over the weekend, and on Monday you will be broke and your family will go lacking for the week. But if I pay you the second half on Monday it will ensure that you return to work and that your family will be taken care of during the week".

Wilmore Jones (1873-?)
Hot Water Businessman and
Farmer   Courtesy – L. Jones

One man that I knew, Mr. Edward Ratcliff, received a US Medal of Honor for leading his company during an attack against a Confederate fort. Mr. Ratcliff was a sergeant in the 36th or 38th Infantry (Colored Troops). They were fighting in a big battle at Chapin's Farm, up near Richmond, Virginia, when the confederates shot down his company commander, a white officer. After the commander was killed, Sergeant Ratcliff led his unit into the fort and captured it. Grandfather said, "Mr. Ratcliff was the first Union Soldier to enter the Confederate Camp."

For this action Sergeant Ratcliff received the US Metal of Honor which is the highest medal given for Bravery in Combat. Mr. Ratcliff told me that when the war was over, his unit was sent to Texas to conduct patrols along the Mexican border. In 1866, the black units were disbanded and the men were sent home. This was an authentic story to my grandfather because his daddy was in the same battle at Richmond, and at the end of the war, his daddy's unit also was sent to Texas. Grandpa said that some of the cavalrymen elected to stay in the army and that they became part of the "Buffalo Soldiers" of the 10th and 15th U.S. Cavalry Regiments.

My daddy told me that when Hot Water was established, it made it a hundred times easier for black slaves to escape to the north. Many times black runaways would come from down south to Richmond and then find their way to Hot Water. Once they arrived in Hot Water, some of the residents would help them make plans to ship themselves up north by boats leaving Jamestown and other places along the James and York River. Often, they were given different clothing and, sometimes, fake passes and other papers that would allow them to move about. Free blacks that lived in Hot Water who could read and write made the passes and other papers. The free blacks had a secret name that they used for Hot Water road. They called it Freedom Road because it and Six Mile Road (Centerville Road) led them to New Jerusalem Road (Brick Bat Road) and finally to Jamestown where slaves could escape to the North by ship or fishing boat to gain their freedom.

Interview with Hazel Pierce Byrd

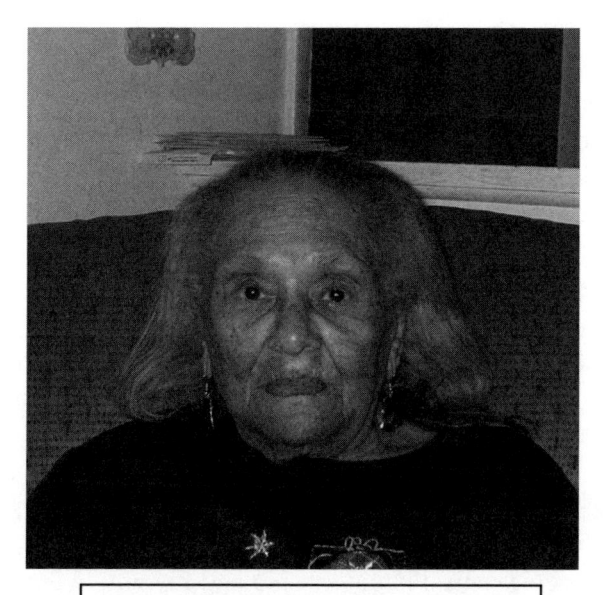

Mrs. Hazel Pierce Byrd, 1916-
Hot Water Resident
Courtesy - L. Jones

"When I was a little girl growing up in "Ziggaboo Town", that's the name my Aunt Calli called Black Stump Landing because only black people lived there, I was a very inquisitive child." Black Stump was located on a little dirt road that intersected with Jolly Pond road, west of the Hot

Water Tract. After my aunt gave it the nickname, almost all of the other black people started calling it that also. The black people used the name affectionately, but they would not use the name around whites because the white people used the name to demean and degrade the black residents both free and slave that lived in the area.

My parents were James and Nora Bell Pierce and there were eleven children in my family. I had four older sisters, Irene, Ocie, Nora and Marrilla, and six brothers, Edward, Percy, Matthew, Sylvester (Shorty), Lloyd and the baby in the family, "Old Jerry". His real name was Henry Clayton Pierce but we called him "Old Jerry" because he was always trying to tell us what to do and what not to do, as if he was our father. He was the family prankster and chief troublemaker. Whenever he started telling one of his tall tales, Daddy would say, "Delaware is at it again." He would say this because Mr. Delaware Brown, who lived nearby was said to be the biggest 'practical jokester' in the county.

Mr. Brown's granddaddy, Mr. Anthony Brown, was a slave at Green Spring Plantation. He and his wife were two of the first slaves freed by William Ludwell-Lee and sent to Hot Water to live. According to Mr. Delaware Brown, his grandfather had eight children. Many of his ancestors continue to live in Williamsburg and James City County today.

My sisters and I spent the majority of our time helping our mother with the laundry and doing other household chores such as cleaning the house, making the beds, milking the cows, collecting eggs from the henhouse and tending the family Garden.

Delaware Brown – Hot Water Resident
Picture taken 1894
Courtesy - L Jones

After we finished our chores, my sisters would go outside to play, but I would stay inside and play by myself until my mother made me go outdoors. This was especially true when the neighbor women came to visit and gossip, "Pass the News", as they would say. I would sit nearby and pretend to be playing with my doll, but I really would be listening to their conversation so I could tell it to my sisters. As a result, I heard all of the latest news and the old stories told by the women. When I heard something that I did not understand, I would remember it and tell it to my sisters so they could explain it to me.

When my grandparents visited, I would get very excited because I knew that I would hear stories about the old days. According to my grandmother, Chris Jane Adkins, my grandpa on my mother's side of the family was Mr. Turner Blanks, a wealthy white merchant from Charles City County, Virginia. In fact, her first four children were born out of wedlock with Mr. Blanks being the father.

Their offspring were my Uncle Shabba "Shang" Adkins, Aunt Mellie Adkins, Aunt Pat Anne Adkins and my mother, Nora Belle Adkins. Their complexions were very fair and were often mistaken for being white. During those days, they could "pass" for white whenever it was necessary.

She later married Richard Richards, a farmer. My maternal grandmother was a small, dark skinned woman. She was very petite with long braids that came down to her waist. She would tell us that part of her family was American Indian and those with fair complexions would tell people that they were mulatto because they were afraid that if the white people thought that they were part Indian, they would lose their farms. Both of their families lived in Charles City and were members of the Chickahominy Indian Tribe.

Shabba "Shang" Adkins, 1873 - 1952
Hot Water Resident
Courtesy - L. Jones

Nora Belle Adkins Pierce 1877 – 1942
Hot Water Resident
Courtesy - L. Jones

My grandmother told me that her father was an Adkins and that he would tell her that his father and grandfather had been tribal chiefs. I don't know how true that was, but I do know that when we visited our family in Charles City and traveled around with them, every one we met were very nice to us, and would give us anything we wanted, if they had it.

My paternal grandfather, William Pierce, was African and lived as a freeman in Hot Water. He was born in 1821 somewhere near Charlottesville, Virginia. I am not sure how he received his freedom, but some people said that his father had fought in the War of 1812, and because of this, he was free. His wife was Simata Pierce, and according to the family, she was Indian and black, and was born in 1826. I do not recall what tribe she was from but I think it was Mattaponi or Pamunkey. I never knew her maiden name, but she told us that her first name meant "Inuit Woman". Their children were Patsy, Sylvester, Victoria, Jolijah, Susan, John, Caledonia and James, my father. The children in my family used to play down near the creek with some of the other kids that lived next door. They were the Joneses, Canadays, and Williams. Sometimes the Wallace kids and some of the white kids that lived up the highway near Jolly Pond road would come down and play with us. The white children said that they could play with us and the Wallace kids because we were all light skinned with slightly curly hair and were referred to as Mustees and Mulattos by the white people. We would play all kinds of games.

Lorraine Jones, my best friend, died when I was about eight years old. We were outside playing one day when she fell down and just started shaking. It was in the summer time and very hot. She stopped shaking for a little while, but by the time her Momma got to where we were, she was shaking again. Her momma took her home and the next day my parents told that she had died. I will never forget that day because it nearly scared the life out of me. At that time, I did not know what had happened, but I did not play outside again when it was hot for a long, long time.

We lived in a big two-story house that had a kitchen to the back. Down stairs were the kitchen, dining room, parlor, living room and two bedrooms. We also had two "root cellars". We put the canned goods and preserves in one of them and potatoes and vegetables in the other. During the summer months, we would preserve many of the vegetables that grew in our garden. We also would dry fruits and vegetables, such as apples, pears, wild grapes and peaches, on the rooftop of our house. My mother would prepare them for natural dehydration and I would take them up on the roof and spread them out to dry. After spreading them out, I would cover then with a piece of thin clothe, very much like cheese-clothe. That was my favorite chore when I was a little girl because I was able to sample everything.

There were three bedrooms upstairs where the children slept. Each room had a small wood stove that we hardly ever used, unless it was unusually cold. The house had fireplaces in the two front rooms and a stove in the kitchen. The heat from downstairs would keep the rooms upstairs reasonably warm during the day, but at night, it got extremely cold.

Miles Cannaday Hot Water Resident
Courtesy - L. Jones

My brothers would take turns putting wood in the fireplace at night when the fires went down. Back then, the winters were very cold and we had lots of snow. Sometimes we would sleep with extra quilts on the bed. At other times, when my brothers got lazy and did not put wood on the fires, it would get so cold that we had to sleep with our clothes on.

Outback we had an outhouse toilet and a smokehouse that was next to the barn. We also had a pigpen, chicken house and dog-pen where my daddy kept his hound dogs. He kept the horses, oxen and cows in the barn.

Our house was different from most of the homes built in Hot Water because it was made from wooden slabs that had been cut at the mill and the roof was made of the same type of boards. I was told that my Grandfather and some of his friends built the house sometime around 1845. The house looked a lot like Segar Bradby's old house over on Centerville Road.

I think the Sawmills were built along the creek and near the freshwater spring so the men and the horses could be close to the water. I also remember the men bringing the logs from Hot Water to Black Stump and floating the logs on the water towards the James River. I do not know if they were taking them to Jamestown or Charles City.

My Mother and some of the women worked as "washer women". They went about their regular jobs as homemakers, but they also washed clothes for the men that worked at the Sawmill and for some of the local white farmers. As I recall, there were two sawmills in the area. One was at Black Stump and the other was in Hot Water near the spring. The spring is behind the house I use to live in on Centerville Road when I was married.

Bradby / Jones Home – in Hot Water. Demolished 2007 ~ Courtesy- L. Jones

According to my husband, Wilton "Monk" Byrd, his family descended from former Green Spring Plantation slaves that were freed during the early 1800's. They lived in the area that people are now calling Hot Water until the 1890's, at which time his family purchased land in Five Forks, where he was born. He also had two Aunts that were former slaves. His Aunt "Tabby" Byrd lived with Mr. "Chicken Crawley. Mr. Crawley's house was back in the woods across the road from the little millpond near New Zion Baptist Church. The old road to his house is still there. His other Aunt, Mrs. Sarah Byrd, lived in a big white house that sat on a hill where the entrance to Ford's Colony is located on Centerville Road. Mr. "Chicken Crawley" also was a descendant of a Greens Spring slave that lived in Hot Water.

On the weekends, some of the families would get together and have cookouts. About half the people came down the creek by boat from Chickahominy. Sometimes they might even come from as far away as Charles City. That way they did not have to worry about the white folks bothering them. Some people would come across the river by boat from Surry and others would come from as far away as Richmond and spend the week with relatives that lived nearby.

There was a good mixture of black people and Indians because we were all mixed up anyway. Some times I would think to myself, "If a real Indian showed up here, all these people would either run away or have a heart attack and die". Many of the "Indians" looked blacker than some of the blacks. The ones that were mixed called themselves Indians when they were among the black people and mulattoes when they were around white people.

According to the old folks, back then, black people and mulattos could own land, but if you were Indian, your land would be taken from you and you would be shipped out of the state, or accidentally killed, if you refused to leave. I do not know personally about anyone that this happened to, but I was told this by several of the older people to include my mother.

At the "get together" the people would have plenty of good food and the men would drink homemade wine and corn whiskey that some of them had made. They also would play baseball and throw horseshoes. Others would just take a break after playing baseball and fish along the creek. Sometimes the men would get lazy, drop a Gillnet across the creek early in the morning, and pull it up sometime around noon. It would be full of all kinds of fish. At other times, some of the men would ride their horses down to James Town and fish in the James River. When they returned, they would clean the fish for the women to cook.

When it started getting dark, the men would light torch fires made from green pine tree branches, kerosene and axle-grease. They also would sprinkle cinnamon on the torches. I do not know if the cinnamon helped keep the bugs away but I do know that the fire smelled better and it seemed to help keep the bugs away. I do know that the torches would burn and put off smoke to drive the mosquitoes away. Sometimes the men would burn other plants to get rid of the insects, but I do not remember what they were.

Sturgeon Fish being sold on Jamestown Pier – Customers at left side of the picture   [Source: APVA]

In addition, there was a group of men that played checkers and chess. This is where my brothers, Shorty and Edward, would spend most of their time. They would walk around and watch the men play. I guess that is why they became two of the best checker and chess players in the county, according to my Daddy. Shorty was so good that you would think he was reading the other player's mind.

He would whisper to us what the other player was going to do at least three to four moves before the other player did it. By the time he was sixteen, the only person that could get lucky and beat him was my brother Edward.

After the sun started setting, the music and dancing would start. This was when we had the most fun. Almost every one, the women, the men, the old folks and the children, would all join in, just dancing and singing up a storm. Some times the children would just sit and laugh at the old people doing all sorts of silly dances. Sometimes the dancing would go on late into the night, and, early in the morning, some of the people would still be awake.

On Sundays, we would all get up early, do our chores and get ready for church. Daddy would hook up one horse to the wagon for us to ride in and he would ride the other horse to church. Either Momma or one of my brothers would drive the wagon. Our church was New Zion Baptist and is still used today. Many family members are there in the cemetery. My Grandparents, parents, all of my brothers and three of my sisters are buried there.

Long before I was born, a little church was built, on the northwest corner, where Black Stump Road intersects with Jolly Pond Road. It was called Angel View Baptist Church. According to Momma, her parents used to go there before New Zion Baptist was constructed. I think Angel View was built in the 1850's or earlier. This is where many of the people that lived in Hot Water attended church. It continued conducting services well into the 1900's, because I attended it a few times with my mother when I was about five or six years old.

The church was very small and had two small rows of benches, a potbelly stove and a small pew. If I remember correctly, it had two windows on each side and a front and back door. There also was an outdoor toilet and a cemetery out back. I do not remember the names of anyone that was buried there, but I am sure that they were all black people.

The church was right across the road from where Aunt Calli and Uncle Wes use to live. They lived on Old Hot Water Road, just east of its intersection with Jolly Pond Road. There was a small cemetery there, however, over the years the different families failed to take care of it.

Sometimes, if the weather were good, my sisters and brothers would walk along Hot Water Road to New Zion Baptist Church. It would take us down past the Bradby/Kennedy Cemetery, across the swamp and over to the intersection of Centerville and Longhill Road. Mr. William "Big Bill" Jones and his brother Mr. Wilmore Jones had houses on Hot Water Road. Mr. "Big Bill" had a two-story house and his brother lived in a single story house.

Do not confuse Mr. Wilmore Jones with his cousin whose name also is Wilmore. His cousin Wilmore Jones lived in the big two-story house over on Centerville Road that had the windmill out back. His wife's name was Mrs. Annie and she was a Dandridge before they married. After his death, she married Mr. Segar Bradby.

There were two cemeteries near their houses. One cemetery was behind their house and the other was just across the road. Two roads formed a fork just west of where the cemeteries were located and then continued as a single road over to Centerville road. The cemetery on the south side of Hot Water Road was the largest and oldest. It had a couple of tombstones, but for the most part, it was overgrown. On the north side of the road was a smaller cemetery. I think some of the Joneses and Wallace's are buried there. The Joneses owned a lot of property in Hotwater and along Jolly Pond and Centerville Roads.

Interview with Lula Howard Lattimore:

Lula Howard Lattimore (1906-2005)
Hot Water Resident. Courtesy-L. Jones

"I do not remember too much about Hot Water that I personally witnessed, but I will tell you what I know and have heard from older people that lived there. Mind you, that is where I grew up as a little girl, but I was married and

moved to Hampton when I was sixteen. From that time on, the only contacts I had with family members were when my husband and I came to visit." As I remember,
"Most of the people that lived there had log cabin homes, except for mamma's 1st cousin, Big Bill Jones, Mr. Jackson, Mr. Harris, some of the Pierces, and my uncle James Jones". "Also, my uncles George, John, and Wilmore Jones had large houses, but I think they bought them from some white people during the 1890's".

My father, Robert H. Howard, was named after his father and grandfather. All of the Howards lived in Hot Water. Almost all of my father's family had small homes. Most of them had small clapboard houses or log cabins that were made from either boards that were cut at the Sawmill or logs that the men had cut and put together. The Howards lived in Hot Water from its very beginning. My great grandfather, Humphrey Howard, was a slave at Green Springs Plantation until he was freed in the early 1800's. After he was freed, he married my great grandma, Matilllda, and they had a bunch of kids. They lived down in 'Jerusalem' until my daddy brought the land up on Centerville Road where my brother, Oscar, had his junkyard. "Jerusalem was the name of a small black neighborhood located on Brick Bat Road near an old abandoned church named New Jerusalem Baptist."

I was born in Hot Water on the east side of Centerville road near its current intersection with Jolly Pond Road. As a little girl, I would travel with my mother, Mary "Marilla" Jones Howard, and her brothers throughout Hot Water and the surrounding area. When they visited the older people in the area, I would listen intently to the stories they told about the civil war and the things that were done by the white people.

According to the stories I heard, some of the white people were very mean and did many hurtful things to the black people, including the free people that lived in Hot Water. They would talk about the hangings and floggings that took place on the different plantations. According to them, some of the white people's ancestors still live in James City County and their attitudes towards black people have not changed much between then and now. For the most part, during the slavery period, they said it was easier here free blacks and slaves than it was in other parts of Virginia and the Deep South. They said that if a Virginia slave were sold in another state the white folks would say that he or she had to be retrained to be a slave because Virginia slaves were too smart and uppity.

"My favorite storyteller was Mr. John Williams who lived on Jolly Pond Road near my uncles George and John Jones' property." He was born into slavery and did not get his freedom until the end of the civil war. His wife, Mrs. Nancy, was born a free woman and was the grand daughter of Mr. Ben Taylor. He was one of the original freed slaves that lived in Hot Water.

Mr. Williams told me that, prior to the civil war, he was owned by Henry Richardson, a white landowner. If I remember correctly, he was born in 1853 and his wife was born in 1854. After gaining their freedom, they became subsistence farmers. They worked their farm by raising crops and pigs that they could sell at the local market. The market was located next door to my father's property at the intersection of Jolly Pond Road and Centerville Road.

Eventually Mr. Williams was able to purchase his own land that was located on Jolly Pond Road next to property owned by my uncles George and John Jones. Later, my uncles sold their property to Matt Pierce and John Henry Neal.

On the other side of my daddy's property were a grocery store, laundry, and blacksmith shop. My uncle, Andrew Jones, owned all three businesses. Later, when cars came into fashion, he converted his blacksmith shop into a garage.

NEWLY FREED SLAVES, THEIR FAMILIES AND THEIR SUCCESSES

Anthony and Rachel Brown

Anthony was a slave freed by William Ludwell-Lee. His wife's name was Rachel and they had seven children. Their names were Mary, Richard, Sicilly (Cecilia), Wesley, Millis, Robert, William and Camillus. County records and the 1850 census list his occupation as farmer and his wife is listed as a washerwoman. The census showed that there were three other adults living with them. They were Rachel's sister Mary, her brother-in-law Robert Skid-more, and her brother William Johnson. Indications are that Anthony Brown did not own his land during the early years and worked as a subsistence farmer for Dandridge Marston, a white landowner.

Ellen Brown, granddaughter of Anthony Brown, and her son
Courtesy - L. Jones

Anthony Brown later acquired his own property and passed it on to his descendents. In the 1850 Census, his son Richardson was listed as being a farmer and another of his sons, Robert, was listed as being a sailor. In addition, his son John Wesley, also known as "Delaware Brown," is listed in the census as being a farmer and having a significant amount of land/assets valued at $500. Richardson brown was one of the first trustees at New Zion Baptist Church. Anthony Brown's descendents continue to live in and adjacent to Hot Water.

William and Maria Cannady (Canaday)

James City County records show that in 1834, William and Maria Cannady was living with their children, Alice, Ann, Delia, Dorcas Eliza, James, Sarah, William, and Zebedia. Maria's sister, Alice Davenport, was also living with them. John was listed in tax records as a subsistence farmer and his wife was listed as a "Coke Seller". By 1860, William had died and his wife was head of household. By 1870, William Cannady, Jr., owned 100 acres of land. His livestock included a milk cow, two oxen, two cows, four pigs and two horses. He also had numerous chickens and ducks. The descendants of this family continue to live in James City County today.

Ben and Lucy Taylor

James City County tax records indicated that in 1832 Ben Taylor was a Free Black male above the age of 16. His brothers, William and David also were free. In 1835, the county tax officer's records showed that Ben Taylor, his wife Lucy and their oldest child, America, were living on land owned by Nathaniel Piggott, a white landowner. Also living with them was a woman named Eliza. By 1836, Ben and his family had moved to the Hot Water Tract. It would appear that they were there for less than a year because tax records show that at some time during 1837 they had moved back to Nathaniel Piggott's land. Records also show that their first son, Henley, was born in 1837. They remained at the Piggott farm through 1838 and, in 1839, Ben's family moved to O.P. Marston's land (Roselynn Farm) located near present day Norge, Virginia. Several other free black families also were working at the Marston property as sharecroppers.

In 1840, the census-taker indicated that Ben shared his home with five other family members. The 1850 census reflected that he owned $200 worth of real estate and listed his children as America, Henley and Patsy Taylor. By 1860, Ben had several additions to his family. He was still married to Lucy and their family additions were recorded as, Mary, Ann, Washington, Amanda, Rebecca, and Rosabella (Rosella). According to county tax records, Ben owned about 100 acres of land. At this time, he was listed as a free black man who owned his property valued at $800 and had personal property valued at $250.

In 1870, Ben and a group of black Baptists wanted to build a neighborhood church on part of the War Hill Tract. Prior to this time, they had been using the New Hope Meeting House for their religious services. The New Hope Meeting House would later become Brown's Baptist Church in honor of Richardson Brown, the son of Anthony Brown, who originally owned the land. In February 1880, Richard L. Henley deeded the church property to Ben Taylor, Moses Harrod, Richardson Brown, Henry Ruffin and John W. Cannaday, Sr. the church trustees. At sometime, in the late 1800's, Brown's Baptist Church was remodeled, and renamed New Zion Baptist Church. The church is located on Long Hill Road, in James City County. Some of Ben Taylor's descendents continue to serve in key positions in the community and the church today.

John and Nancy Jackson, Sr.

John Jackson became a Freedman in 1804. His family consisted of his wife Nancy and his children Eliza, Susan, Jacob, Leticia and Marcus. Early tax records showed that by 1811 he had obtained a horse, a wagon, and six cows. In addition, County Tax and Land records show that by 1823, John Jackson, Sr., had become a successful farmer and were able to purchase 100 acres of land from the John Drummond Estate. This property was directly across Centerville road from the Hot Water Tract. Today, the housing complex known as Mulberry Place is on a part of his original property.

During the 1830's several other black families moved to John Jackson's property and worked his lands as sharecroppers. This enabled him to acquire additional finances to purchase more land.

In 1834, his brother, James Jackson, Sr., was living on his land along with his family but in a separate house from John's family. A year later, James and his wife moved to his father-in-law's property. There were three houses on John's property. Periodically members of his extended family lived in these houses. In 1838, John Jackson purchased another 12 acres from Charles Green. This land was adjacent to the New Hope Meeting House.

By 1840, John Jackson had become the second wealthiest black landowner in James City County. The value of his buildings and other assets earned him a place along side the middle class whites.

Following John Jackson's death in 1867, his estate was divided among his sons, Marcus and Jacob, and his daughters, Nancy (Mrs. Edward Ned Davis), Eliza (Mrs. James Cole) and Leticia (Mrs. Samuel Crawley), and his grandson George Jackson. Members of the Jackson family also resided in Ware Creek, another free black settlement that evolved independently about the same time as Hot Water. In 1891, Nancy sold 23 acres to her nephew, Jeremiah Wallace. Descendents of the Cole, Crawley and Jackson family continue to live in the Williamsburg area near Hot Water.

Archer and Mary Wallace (Wallis)

One of the most interesting Free-Blacks was Archer Wallace also known as Archer Wallis. In 1833, he was taxed for owning 38.75 acres of land that had been left to him by his parents, John and Sarah Wallace. However, in 1834 records show that he and his wife Mary were living in the household of his brother-in-law, Thomas Gaines.

Thomas, his wife Edith (Eady) and his brother-in-law, David (Davy) Taylor was listed as living on the property belonging to Dandridge Marston. He was listed as being a subsistence farmer and his wife Edith was a laundress. David Taylor was later shown as a property owner in Ware creek. By 1835, Archer Wallace had moved his family to his own land. The 1850 Census showed his family consisted of his wife and their children. Their children were William, Richard, Susan, Adeline, James, Martha and George.[67] It also showed that he owned $90 worth of real estate. By 1860, his net value had increased and records show that he owned $100 worth of real estate and $120 of personal property.

The James City County Agricultural records for 1860 revealed that 20 acres of his original 38.75 had been improved. At this time, his farm was valued at $114. His livestock included a horse, a milk cow, two oxen and eight pigs. Records also showed that in 1869 he had produced a significant amount of products for sale at the local markets. Records and sales receipts show that he had produced five bushels of Indian corn, twenty bushels of Irish potatoes, a hundred pounds of butter and h e had sold $100 worth of meat, forty gallons of milk and produced another $120 worth of other products."[68]

Numerous extensions of this family exist today in James City County and are making significant contributions to the community and the state of Virginia. Descendents of Archer Wallace continue to live in the nearby communities of Grove, Williamsburg and in York County, Virginia.

DESCENDENTS OF ORIGINAL HOT WATER RESIDENTS - 1920

Robert Adkins	Oscar Howard	Duga Richards
Sarah Adkins	Willie Boy Howard	Marie Richards
Robert Adkins, Jr.	Missouri Green	Fluanna Richards
Elizabeth Adkins	Lawrence Green	John Richards
Shabba Adkins	* Billie Giles	Arthur Richards
Pinky Adkins	William "Big Bill" Jones	Coleman & Gracie Richardson (White)
Ida Adkins	Ida Jones	Willie Saunders
Signor Bradby	John Jones	James Tabb
Cephas Bradby	Sarah Jones	Ben Taylor
Charles Bradby	Wilmore & Annie Jones	Edward Taylor
Porterfield Bradby	James Jones	Henley Taylor
Peter Brown	James W. Jones, Sr.	Fred Taylor, Sr.
Ellis & Laura Burgess	James W. Jones, Jr.	Fred Taylor, Jr.
Willie Brown	Elizabeth Jones	Percy Taylor
Mr. Bowman	Spencer Minor & Family (White)	Lucy Taylor
Miles Cannaday	Caledonia Pierce	Mandy Taylor
McKinley Cannady	Cassius Pierce	Burley Wallace
Willis Cannady	John Pierce	John Williams Robert Williams
William Canady & Family	Arthur Pierce	Caddy Wyatt
Irvin Chandler	James & Nora Bell Pierce	Duga Wyatt
"Chicken" Crawley	Jolijah Pierce	Henry "Cocky" Wyatt
Major Fisher	Chris Ann & Richard Richards	Marie Wyatt
Irvin Chandler	Christopher Richards	Martha Wyatt
Mr. Cumber	Willis Richards	Fluanna Wyatt
Connie Harrison (Harris) & Family		Helen Wyatt
Will & Bell Howard		Mandy Wyatt
Lula Howard		
Clara Howard		

CONCLUSION

A book such as this, dealing with historical information relative to the institution of slavery and its effects on African American lives, deserves the best that an author can give. The successes of the Freedmen in Hot Water are examples of great victories against unfavorable odds and should serve as inspiration to the descendents of these early African Americans.

It also serves as a tribute to my great, great grandfather, the freedmen of Hot Water, and the hundreds of thousands of African Americans that followed them into an existence where they were not the true masters of their own destinies. Today, we take for granted many of the simple, basic privileges that they were denied. A closer examination of their triumphs will show that these men and women were more that just a group of freedmen and former slaves; they were the beginning of a powerful union of different races that have not yet reached its heights.

Footnotes

[1] Heinegg, Paul, Free African Americans in North Carolina, Virginia, and South Carolina, Clearfield Company, 2001.
[2] Hughes, Sarah and Zeigler, J. *Jamestown's Other People*, Children's Program Teachers Manual, Colonial National Historical Park, 1976.
[3] Ibid
[4] Pace, Noble H. Pace, One of America's Oldest Immigrant Families, Published by Pace Society.
[5] Bennett, Lerone Jr., The Shaping of Black America, Johnson Publishing Company (1975) p.7
[6] Franklin, John Hope, Black Americans, Time-Life Books, 1970, page 12.
[7] Ibid
[8] Woolley, Benjamin, SAVAGE KINGDOM: The True Story of Jamestown, 1607, And the Settlement of America, Publisher HarperCollins.
[9] Kupperman, Karen Ordahl, THE JAMESTOWN PROJECT, Publisher Harvard University.
[10] Thorndale, William, William,
[11] Kupperman, Karen Ordahl, THE JAMESTOWN PROJECT, Publisher Harvard University.
[12] Bennett, Lerone Jr., The Shaping of Black America, Johnson Publishing Company (1975), p.152
[13] Ibid, p. 148.
[14] Slaves Virtually Free in Antebelleum North Carolina, The Journal of Negro History Vol 28, No. 3 (Jul 1943) pp 284-310, doi 10.2307/2714910.
[15] Ibid
[16] Ibid
[17] Berlin, Ira. Slaves Without Masters: The Free Negro in the Antebellum South. New York: Pantheon Books, 1974
[18] Slavery in the Colonial Chesapeake: The Foundations of America. Williamsburg, Virginia: Colonial Williamsburg Foundation, 1986.
[19] Ibid and Family Oral History.
[20] Eaton, Clement, "Slave Hiring in the Upper South: A Step Toward Freedom, "Mississippi Valley Historical Review 46 (March 1960).

[21] Walsh, "Slave Life, Slave Society,"191; Thomas C. Buchanan, Black Life on the Mississippi: Slaves, Free Blacks, and Western Steamboat World (Chapel Hill, 2004), 21.
[22] Ibid
[23] Ibid
[24] Starobin, Robert S., Industrial Slavery in the Old South (New York, 1970), 135; Eaton, Clement, "Slave Hiring in the Upper South: A Step Toward Freedom, "Mississippi Valley Historical Review 46 (March 1960), 672; Berlin, Ira, Generations of Captivity: A History of North-American Slaves (Cambridge, 2003), 223; Boles, John B., Black Southerners, 1619-1869 (Lexington, 1984), 129.
[25] Wood, *Women's Work, Men's Work*, 129; Takagi, *"Rearing Wolves to Our Own Destruction"*, 118-121
[26] Dew, Charles B., Bond of Iron: Master and Slave at Buffalo Forge, (New York, 1994), p. 183-185.
[27] Ibid
[28] Ibid.
[29] Heinegg, Paul, "Free African Americans in North Carolina, Virginia, and South Carolina
[30] Heinegg, Paul, "Free African Americans in North Carolina, Virginia, and South Carolina, Clearfield Company, 2001.
[31] Ibid.
[32] Henning, William W. Ed. The Statues at Large: Being a Collection of all Laws of Virginia, from the first session of the Legislature in the year 1619. 13 Volumes Richmond, New York and Philadelphia, 1809-1823.
[33] Ibid
[34] Henning, William W. Ed. *The Statues at Large: Being a Collection of all Laws of Virginia, from the first session of the Legislature in the year 1619.* 13 Volumes Richmond, New York and Philadelphia, 1809-1823.
[35] Ibid
[36] June Purcell Guild, LL.M, "The Black Laws of Virginia," Whittet & Shepperson, 1936.
[37] McCartney, Martha W., "History of Green Spring Plantation", 1998; and " James City County: Keystone of the Commonwealth", Donning Publishing Company, Virginia Beach, Virginia.

[38] Thornton, John, "The African Experience of the 20 and Odd Negroes Arriving in Virginia in 1619." William & Mary Quarterly; Vol. LV, July 1998, No. 3.

[39] Heinegg, Paul, "Free African Americans in North Carolina, Virginia, and South Carolina, Clearfield Company, 2001.

[40] Ibid. Pgs 76-77

[41] Heinegg, Paul, "Free African Americans in North Carolina, Virginia, and South Carolina, Tate, Thad W., The Negro in Eighteenth-Century Williamsburg.

[42] Ibid.

[43] Tate, Thad W., The Negro in Eighteenth-Century Williamsburg.

[44] Bogger, Tommy L., Since 1776: The History of First Baptist Church, Williamsburg, Virginia

[45] Ibid

[46] McCartney, Mary, An African American Heritage Trails Project: The Free Black Community at Centerville, James City County, Virginia, 2000.

[47] Family Oral History

[48] Ibid

[49] Earnest, Joseph B. Jr., The Religious Development of the Negro in Virginia, Charlottesville: Mitchie Company, 1914.

[50] The Virginia Gazette, July 1949.

[51] Ibid

[52] McCartney, Martha W., "History of Green Spring Plantation", 1998; and " James City County: Keystone of the Commonwealth", Donning Publishing Company, Virginia Beach, Virginia.

[53] Ibid

[54] Ibid

[55] Lee, William Ludwell, "1802 Will", "Letters, 1769-1802", Rockefeller Library, Colonial Williamsburg Foundation, Williamsburg, Virginia.

[56] Family Oral History

[57] Ibid

[58] Ibid

[59] McCartney, Martha W., "History of Green Spring Plantation", 1998; and " James City County: Keystone of the Commonwealth", Donning Publishing Company, Virginia Beach, Virginia.

[60] Family Oral History. Blacks commonly refer to this area today as Jerusalem.

[61] McCartney, Martha W., "History of Green Spring Plantation", 1998; and " James City County: Keystone of the Commonwealth", Donning Publishing Company, Virginia Beach, Virginia.

[62] Heinegg, Paul, "Free African Americans in North Carolina, Virginia, and South Carolina, Clearfield Company, 2001.

[63] James City County, Virginia, Land Records, Tax Records, and Census records, 1790 to 1880, James City County Courthouse, Williamsburg, Virginia and Library of Virginia, Richmond, Virginia.

[64] Ibid and Oral History

[65] Oral History of George Jones

[66] Ibid

[67] 1850 Census. James City County, Virginia.

[68] McCartney, Martha W., "History of Green Spring Plantation", 1998; and " James City County: Keystone of the Commonwealth", Donning Publishing Company, Virginia Beach, Virginia. [68] Pace, Noble H. Pace, One of America's Oldest Immigrant Families, Published by Pace Society.

SOURCES:

Bennett, Lerone Jr., "Before the Mayflower: A History of Black America", sixth edition; and The Shaping of America, Johnson Publishing Company, Chicago, 1975.

Berlin, Ira. "Many Thousands Gone, The First Two Centuries of Slavery in North America." Harvard University Press, 1998.

Berlin, Ira. Slaves Without Masters: The Free Negro in the Antebellum South. New York: Pantheon Books, 1974

Billings, Warren M. Ed., *The Old Dominion in the Seventeenth Century - A Documentary History of Virginia, 1606-1689.* University of North Carolina Press, 1975

Breen, T.H., and Innes, S. *Myne Owne Ground: Race and Freedom in Virginia's Eastern Shore, 1640-1676.* New York: Oxford University Press: 1980.

Craven, Wesley F. *White, Red and Black: The Seventeenth Century Virginian*, Charlottesville, 1961.

E. Salmon & E. Campbell, Jr. Eds. "The Hornbook of Virginia History" - 4th Edition, 1994

Gilmer, J.F., Maps, 1863, 1864, 1865 and 1867, Vicinity of Richmond and Parts of the Peninsula, including the Counties of New Kent, Charles City and James City, National Archives, Washington, D.C.

Heinegg, Paul, "Free African Americans in North Carolina, Virginia, and South Carolina, Clearfield Company, 2001.

Henning, William W. Ed. _The Statues at Large: Being a Collection of all Laws of Virginia, from the first session of the Legislature in the year 1619._ 13 Volumes Richmond, New York and Philadelphia, 1809-1823.

Hughes, Sarah and Zeigler, J. _Jamestown's Other People, Children's Program Teachers Manual_, Colonial National Historical Park, 1976.

Hotten, James C., "The Original Lists of Persons of Quality, 1600-1700", British State Paper Office, published 1874.

James City County, Virginia, Land Records, Tax Records, and Census records, 1790 to 1880, James City County Courthouse, Williamsburg, Virginia and Library of Virginia, Richmond, Virginia.

Jones, Jacqueline, "American Work - Four Centuries of Black & White Labor." W.W. Norton & Company, 1998.

June Purcell Guild, LL.M, "The Black Laws of Virginia," Whittet & Shepperson, 1936.

Kulikoff, Allan, "Tobacco and Slaves, The Development of Southern Cultures in the Cheasapeake, 1680-1800.

Lee, William Ludwell, "1802 Will", "Letters, 1769-1802", Rockefeller Library, Colonial Williamsburg Foundation, Williamsburg, Virginia.

Mary A. Stephenson, Notes on a Negro School in Williamsburg, 1760-1774, unpublished research report, Colonial Williamsburg Foundation, June 1964, p. 4.

McCartney, Martha W., "History of Green Spring Plantation", 1998; and " James City County: Keystone of the Commonwealth", Donning Publishing Company, Virginia Beach, Virginia.

Morgan, Philip D. "Slave Counterpoint Black Culture in the 18th Century Chesapeake & Low Country," University of North Carolina Press, 1998.

Thorndale, William, "The Virginia Census of 1619," Magazine of Virginia Genealogy, Vol. 33, Summer 1995, No. 3. (See Mary W. McCartney's article "An Early Virginia Census Reprised" for another discussion on the date of the census that she places in 1620)

Thornton, John, "The African Experience of the 20 and Odd Negroes Arriving in Virginia in 1619." William & Mary Quarterly; Vol. LV, July 1998, No. 3.

Vaughan, Alden T. *"Blacks in Virginia: A Note on the First Decade"* The William and Mary Quarterly, XXIX, July 1972.

William and Mary Quarterly, 1st ser., vol. 20, p. 171; Ibid. vol. 27, pp. 107-108; *Virginia Magazine of History and Biography*, vol. 3, p. 427; and Ibid., vol. 8, p. 257.

WPA, "The Negro in Virginia," Publisher, John F. Blair, 1994.